Dedication

This book is dedicated to my Lord and Savior, Jesus Christ, who loves me enough to discipline me when I need it. I also make special dedication to the memory of my father, Nathaniel Hawthorne Bronner, Sr., who loved me enough to discipline me when I needed it.

GET A GRIP

(How To Handle The Seven Toughest Problems Of Life)

By

Dale Carnegie Bronner

Acknowledgments

I give special thanks to my oldest brother, Nathaniel Bronner Jr., who encouraged me to write this book. I thank Stanley Ferrell with IN-Line Graphics for the artistic elements he added to the book. I thank Traci Bronner and Lee Bliss for lending their editorial skills. Thanks also to my precious family for their patience, love and understanding throughout this project. Finally, I wish to thank all the wonderful members of Word Of Faith Family Worship Center for their love and support.

The old saying states, "Opportunity only knocks once." If this is true, you should hurry to the door even when you suspect you hear the sound of a knock.

The old saying states, "Opportunity only knocks once." If this is true, you should hurry to the door even when you suspect you hear the sound of a knock. Better still, if you are prepared for the opportunity, you should be looking out the window expecting the opportunity to come. There is nothing more frustrating than to have a golden opportunity that you are not prepared to receive. So what is the logical thing to do? Get as thoroughly prepared as possible. Why take a chance on not being ready? The old folks used to say, "You never get a second chance to make a first impression."

If you have ever had to refuse an opportunity because you were not prepared, you should be determined not to allow that to happen again. Preparation requires change, but because we are creatures of habit, we hate to change. Yet, you cannot afford to be afraid of change, expansion or development. To the contrary, you must welcome change as an opportunity for improvement. So as you read this book, open up your mind and expand your horizons.

An open mind is a mind that welcomes change and diversity. On the other hand, a closed mind is a mind that is stagnant and will never rise above the level of mediocrity. When you open your mind, though, you must be discriminating about what you permit to enter. Sift through ideas and thoughts and only accept the good, positive ones. You have to learn to "eat the fish and throw away the bones!" To assist in this, I have made every attempt to "filet" this book for you!

Just as you should be selective of your nutritional diet, you should be selective of your mental and spiritual diet. You only want to imbibe that which will be good, nutritious "food for thought." Remember, you are what you eat. So if your mind ingests trash, you will think trashy thoughts, speak trashy words and act out trashy behaviors.

When you eat mental food, you have to take your time in digesting it. Think on it. Meditate about it. This will yield understanding or further revelation which will benefit your entire being. Just as eating slower allows the cells to absorb maximum nutrition from the food, this works the same way. So when you partake of a mental or spiritual diet, be sure to take small portions at a time. Chew them slowly, or else you will develop mental or spiritual indigestion. Because the average person does not know how much of a good thing is too much, you need to consciously establish boundaries for yourself. This book is designed to help you do just that. These boundaries are not for the purpose of restricting your life, but rather to help you organize and protect it!

An open mind realizes that organizing your life relieves stress. An open mind that is fed with good thoughts always looks on the bright side of life and is full of hope. A closed mind is a hopeless mind. A hopeless mind is a helpless mind. But as long as your mind remains open, you can stay in motion and see a way out of every situation!

An open mind listens for a knock at the door. It is ready for a new opportunity. It is ready to be improved. It does not prejudge situations. Rather, it listens to get all the facts so judgment will be more precise. When you open your mind, you remove limitations that hinder your progress.

Open your mind to growth, prosperity and success. Think big thoughts and entertain big ideas, but implement them on a small basis first. Expect good things, and they will come. Instead of living with a "business as usual" attitude, dare to open your mind and meet the needs of the time. Instead of trying to be a "big fish in a small pond," open your mind to the great sea of life! Instead of having the mentality of being the best in your family or class or race or nation, think of being the best in the world!

To be the best in anything, you must have good discipline. *Get A Grip* is written to help you develop better discipline in your life. An 8 year old creative writing student, Myles Spence, wrote, "If you're not disciplined at home, youíre disciplined at school. If you're not disciplined at school, you're disciplined on the streets. If you're not disciplined on the streets, you're disciplined in jail. If you're not disciplined there, time's up, you're in hell!" Clearly the point is that if you are not disciplined early, you'll pay a severe penalty to learn a valuable lesson later. As you read this book, keep your mind open, or you will shut out much more than you are shutting in! *"Whoever loves discipline loves knowledge, but he who hates reproof is stupid"* (Prov. 12:1 NAS).

CHAPTER 1
Dead Meat

"My (sex) drive is just too high."

C O N T E N T S

Preface

Recently, a well groomed 63-year-old woman came into my office for counseling. I could not imagine what her need was. She came in, sat down and after a few seconds said, "I don't know how to begin." Smiling, I looked over at this impeccably dressed, silver-haired woman and light-heartedly said, "You begin by simply sharing why you think you needed to come today."

Taking deep breaths and sighing several times, she softly admitted, "I have a problem with my sex drive!" Looking over my desk at this pristine woman, I immediately thought she was about to tell me, "I just don't have a desire for sex." But before I could complete what was racing through my mind, she clarified herself stating, "My (sex) drive is just too high." With self-analysis she continued, "I feel abnormal. This just isn't right for a woman my age! I can't even go a full day without thinking about sex." Trying to explain her dilemma she concluded, "I believe the devil is making me crave sex!" Then with deep embarrassment she dropped her head and softly solicited, "Will you please pray for me so that these feelings will leave me and never bother me again?" Without bursting her bubble of hope, I replied, "I wish it were that simple. But it will take more than prayer to bring this under control."

During the first few minutes of our conversation, I thought the woman was married; I really did not see the big problem she had. But then she revealed, "What makes it so bad is that I'm divorced,   but sometimes I still call my ex-husband (who is remarried) and sleep with him. Plus I have other boyfriends with whom I sleep. But now I am plagued with guilt and shame." She went on, "I know I need to stop, but I can't seem to help myself. Men are just my weakness!" I tried to console her a little by saying, "Although your flesh is weak, I'm sure your spirit is willing to try to obey God."

For nearly the next 45 minutes, I looked to the Scriptures to bring understanding to this woman's situation. I sincerely wanted her to understand who and what she was fighting against.   So I began by turning to the book of Galatians:

For the flesh lusteth against the Spirit, and the Spirit against the flesh: and these are contrary the one to the other: so that ye cannot do the things that ye would.
Galatians 5:17

For the desires of the flesh are opposed to the (Holy) Spirit, and the [desires of the] Spirit are opposed to the flesh (Godless human nature); for these are antagonistic to each other — continually withstanding and in conflict with each other — so that you are not free but are prevented from doing what you desire to do.
Galatians 5:17 (AMP)

The whole idea of this verse is to point out that the flesh wars against the Holy Spirit who dwells us. Then the bible lists some works of the flesh:

*Now the works of the flesh are manifest, which are these; **ADULTERY, FORNICATION,** uncleanness, lasciviousness, idolatry, witchcraft, hatred, variance, emulations, wrath, strife, seditions, heresies, envyings, murders, drunkenness, revellings, and such like; of the*

which I tell you before, as I have also told you in the past, that they which do such things shall not inherit the kingdom of God.
Galatians 5:19-21

Notice that this passage says nothing at all about these things being "works of the devil" or of demons or some evil spirit. These things are works of the flesh! **You cannot have someone pray for you and cast out a spirit of adultery or fornication or hatred because these are works of your flesh. They are not a direct work of the devil, although he is ultimately responsible for appealing to your flesh.**

It is helpful for you to understand that your flesh is the only part of you that is not born again. You renew your mind with the Word of God. Your spirit is born again, but your flesh is not! So unless you get your mind renewed with the Word of God, your flesh will dominate you. Your flesh is born in sin and shaped in iniquity. Your flesh will never lose that sin nature. Your spirit can lose its sin nature, but not your flesh. There are still works of evil that abide in your flesh. So you cannot pray or cast out a demon in these areas that are works of the flesh! **By the discipline of your spirit and mind, you must take control of your flesh and keep it under subjection.**

You cannot cast out a demon of fornication from a teenager and think he will no longer desire to have sex. Fornication is a work of the flesh! You must understand whose work it is before you can control the work. A married woman cannot anoint her suspicious husband with oil and drive out a "spirit of adultery." That is a direct work of human flesh. Please do not get me wrong, there are evil spirits for whom you can open the door to your life. These demonic spirits may then drive you to obsessive behavior in sexual affairs or some other illicit activity. Certain deeds of the flesh open the door to demonic spirits. But most people are not demon-possessed. They simply have uncontrolled fleshly desires.

Your life is like a garden. You plant seeds in your life and up they come. You sow, you reap a harvest. Of course, you may sow wonderful seeds in the garden of your heart. But if you do not control your terrain, the devil will bring up all kinds of weeds to destroy your garden. If you do not pull up the weeds to control wild growth, the weeds will choke out the life of the seeds of productive things you planted. Our garden is to be dedicated for the use of good, productive plants. Anything else should be discarded.

"... Every plant, which my heavenly Father hath not planted, shall be rooted up" (Matthew 15:13).

To keep our flesh from wrecking havoc in our lives, we have to take control over the bad tendencies and influences. **We cannot afford to play with fire and expect never to be burned.** We ought to reserve all our territory for the Lord. *"Neither give place to the devil" (Ephesians 4:27).* God wants all of us, and He deserves to have us to Himself.

And thou shalt love the Lord thy God with all thy heart, and with all thy soul, and with all thy mind, and with all thy strength: this is the first commandment.
Mark 12:30

In other words, God is saying, "I want you to love me with every part of you." You cannot say, "Lord, I have given you my heart, mind and soul, but this body belongs to me!" No, you have to give God all of you.

Regardless of how saved, anointed or spiritual you are, you must realize that you are wrapped in unredeemed, unregenerate human flesh. People have been casting out "alcohol and nicotine spirits" for years. But I am not convinced that everybody who drinks is possessed with an "alcoholic devil." Likewise, I am not convinced that everyone who smokes is possessed by a "nicotine devil." I neither drink nor smoke. I never have. I never will. I am not advocating smoking or drinking. But notice from the scriptural list of works of the flesh that "drunkenness" is named as a work of the flesh. Of course that word "drunkenness" also encompasses inebriation caused by drugs. So that means you cannot just cast out a spirit and set free everyone who drinks or does drugs.

Don't misunderstand me. Drinking and doing drugs can open the door to Satan for addiction and demonic bondage. But it all starts as a work of the flesh. I have been privileged to see some people miraculously delivered, by the sovereignty and mercy of God, who were addicted to drugs and/or alcohol. Yet even after deliverance, they had to change their environment and submit themselves to prayer and the Word of God to transform their mind and control the fleshly desire for drugs.

If we can learn to head off sin as a work of the flesh, we will not have a need for spiritual deliverance in many instances. The devil knows that once you have committed your heart to the Lord, the only way he can contact you is through your flesh! He will torment you by causing you to worry about how you are going to take care of **your** flesh. So when the devil wants to bring you down, all he has to do is whisper something to your flesh. All he has to do is bring up ungodly desires in your flesh. But remember, the devil uses works of your flesh to cause you to stumble!

We love to relegate everything negative to a foul, evil spirit. We always look for someone else to take the blame for our wrong. We are not the first to do that, and we will not be the last. Remember, Adam first practiced "buck passing" when he blamed his disobedience on his wife, Eve. Then Eve shifted responsibility to the serpent. But God held each person responsible for his own actions. We sometimes act like we have a case of the "can't help its," but the truth is that we do not want to help it! We want to find someone to blame for our savage desires. If you really want to know who to blame, get a mirror! You will discover that it is your flesh that is at war with the Spirit.

You may sit down to read your Bible or to pray, when all of a sudden, your flesh gets sleepy. Well, you can rebuke the devil all you want, but you will still be sleepy. Do you know why? Because your flesh is warring against the Spirit! It is not directly the devil. Of course the devil is using your flesh to destroy your spirit.

Because we are in a physical world (and the devil is the god of this world [II Corinthians 4:4]), he can contact us through our physical flesh. Whenever I get sleepy while praying or reading my Bible, I just stand up and walk around for a while. Or I will open a window and let in some fresh air. You see, I have to take the initiative to do something about my own flesh. That is my responsibility. God made me the custodian of this body in which I live. So I have to control it.

That ye put off concerning the former conversation the old man, which is corrupt according to the deceitful lusts; and be renewed in the spirit of your mind; and that ye put on the new man, which after God is created in righteousness and true holiness.

Ephesians 4:22-24

Yes, it is **your** responsibility, not God's, to strip yourself of the "old man" (fleshly nature) and put on the "new man," which is created in righteousness and holiness. Then it is your responsibility to be **renewed in the spirit of your mind.** What you watch on television feeds the spirit of your mind. The music you listen to feeds the spirit of your mind. The books you read feed the spirit of your mind. The conversations you pay attention to impact the spirit of your mind. So we must learn to be very discriminating with what we expose our minds to. I do not believe there is any way you can look at sex on television and at the movies, listen to its lyrics in music and read its passionate eroticism in novels without getting "sex on the brain." You can control what renews your mind. You control what you put on and what you pull off.

God does not "pull off" and "put on" for you. He will encourage and help you, but you are responsible for following his instructions. God told the people what to "pull off," so that means they had it on. Then He told them to "put on" because they obviously had "off" something of importance. In Colossians, instead of using "pull off," Paul uses the word "mortify." Mortify literally means to put to death or kill. But the practical application of "mortify" means to subdue. We do not want to kill our flesh literally. We just want to subdue it so we can control it.

Mortify, therefore, your members which are upon the earth; fornication, uncleanness, inordinate affection, evil concupiscence, and covetousness, which is idolatry ... And put on the new man, which is renewed in knowledge after the image of him that created him ... Put on, therefore, as the elect of God, holy and beloved, bowels of mercies, kindness, humbleness of mind, meekness, longsuffering.
Colossians 3:5,10,12

The truth is Christians have much more trouble with their flesh than they do directly with the devil! Many Christians have a big problem trying to keep their lusts under control.

Lust rises out of our own being. By the way, in several societies, women are made to conceal almost everything except their eyes. The head is covered. The arms are covered. The legs are covered. Loosely layered clothing is worn over the body so as not to reveal a shape. The mouth is even covered. This "covering" is not done to protect the woman's modesty, but to hinder

an opportunity for a man to lust. Instead of transform-
ing the mind of the one who is prone to lust, they simply
lock up and cover up the object of the man's lust. To me,
that is merely treating a symptom and not the root cause
of the problem. **Whatever we refuse to confront can
never be conquered! Either we begin controlling our
lusts or our lusts will control and, inevitably, destroy
us!**

*Wherefore God also gave them up to uncleanness [a
work of the flesh] through the lusts of their own hearts,
to dishonour their own bodies between themselves ... For
this cause God gave them up unto vile affections: for
even their women did change the natural use into that
which is against nature: And likewise also the men,
leaving the natural use of the woman, burned in their
lust one toward another; men with men working that
which is unseemly, and receiving in themselves that rec-
ompence of their error which was meet. And even as
they did not like to retain God in their knowledge, God
gave them over to a reprobate mind, to do those things
which are not convenient.*
                Romans 1:24, 26-28

Does this passage say anything about the devil's lust?
No, it talks about the lust of the individual. Then when
lust goes uncontrolled, it leads to mental reprobation. A
reprobate mind is a mind void of judgment. That is
when your mind no longer judges you. You are no
longer convicted for wrongdoing. Thus if you are not
convicted, you will never seek forgiveness in that area.
This is a dangerous condition to be in, spiritually.

Remember that Christians will have more trouble with their flesh than they will directly with the devil or demons. I Peter 2:11 admonishes that we *"abstain from fleshly lusts, which war against the soul."* Again there is no mention of *"demonic lusts,"* but of **"fleshly lusts."**

Some Christians have trouble with their tongues. They gossip and say derogatory things about people. Yet, they cannot simply change because they get in someone's prayer line to have it "cast out of them." You see, your tongue is an unruly part of your **flesh!** You cannot stand back and say, "The devil made me say that!"

*But every man is tempted, when he is drawn away of his **own lust**, and enticed. Then when lust hath conceived, it bringeth forth sin: and sin, when it is finished, bringeth forth death.*

James 1:14-15

*Among whom also we all had our conversation in times past in the **lusts of our flesh**, fulfilling the **desires of the flesh** and of the mind; and were by nature the children of wrath, even as others.*

Ephesians 2:3

Can you see that it is not the lust of the devil, but the **lust of the flesh?** Lust is a part of our unregenerate flesh. **Lust is nothing more than pleasure of the flesh.** When you think about it, **everything we lust after is something we think will give pleasure to our flesh.**

So how do we deal with this lusty flesh of ours? Do we just pray and hope that it does not bother us? Do we seek to cover up the object of our lust? Do we pluck out

our eyes? Do we run away from it? Of course not! So
what do we do? *"...Walk in the Spirit, and ye shall not
fulfill the lust of the flesh" (Galatians 5:16). "And they
that are Christ's have crucified the flesh with the affections and lusts. If we live in the Spirit, let us also walk
in the Spirit"* *(Galatians 5:24-25).*

Exactly what does it mean to "walk in the Spirit"? I
believe that "walking in the (Holy) Spirit" is synonymous with exemplifying the "fruit of the (Holy) Spirit."
When you practice **love, joy, peace, longsuffering, gen-
tleness, goodness, faith(fulness), meekness and tem-
perance,** you are walking in the Spirit (Galatians 5:22-
23). But you cannot walk in the Spirit without crucify-
ing the flesh. You have to have **"dead meat."** When you
exercise control over your lusts, it will sometimes feel as
if it is "killing" you. But that is just your flesh being
crucified. It is hard, but you can do it! Do not think
about it. Just do it! Crucify your flesh and realize that
death precedes every resurrection. So when you die to
your fleshly desires, you are raised to new life in the
Spirit.

Every time you are tempted to do wrong, imagine
yourself on the cross with Jesus. See the crown of
thorns, pressing down in the tender scalp of Jesus, causing blood to trickle down his face. See the grimace on
his face, with his teeth clinched tightly together, as 5
inch stakes are driven through his hands and feet. See
the sun dehydrating his body. See the lacerations on his
back from the whips. See his weakened body dangling
with his weight pulling against the nails. See the profuse
blood loss. Then see in his eyes the determination to

crucify his flesh and take away sin to bring spiritual redemption. At any cost, Jesus was willing to pay the price to crucify his flesh. With Jesus as our example, we must be willing to do the same.

Knowing this, that our old man is crucified with him, that the body of sin might be destroyed, that henceforth we should not serve sin. For he that is dead is freed from sin ... Likewise reckon ye also yourselves to be dead indeed unto sin, but alive unto God through Jesus Christ our Lord. Let not sin therefore reign in your mortal body, that ye should obey it in the lusts thereof. Neither yield ye your members as instruments of unrighteousness unto sin: but yield yourselves unto God, as those that are alive from the dead, and your members as instruments of righteousness unto God. For sin shall not have dominion over you: for ye are not under the law, but under grace.

Romans 6:6-7,11-14

The wonderful thing about considering yourself to be dead is knowing that a dead person has no temptations. When you are dead, **sin shall not have dominion over you!** It would be a blessing for you to make that statement personal by confessing, **"Sin shall not have dominion over me!"** If you become involved with sin, it will become your master. Then sin dictates the time to get drunk, the time to fornicate or the time to tell a lie and gossip. The above passage was written to the Church at Rome. You see, they had big problems controlling their flesh at the Church in Rome, in Ephesus, in Galatia, in Corinth, in Colosse and everywhere else people were found. And we still have a big problem with our flesh in the Church today. But thank God we are learning how to control the flesh, instead of letting it rule us!

CHAPTER 2

What You See Is
What You Want

"If you get your eyes off the "greenness"
of your neighbor's grass, you can appreciate your grass more."

Among the many profound thoughts that William Shakespeare penned, one particularly stands out in my mind. He said, **"Happiness is not having what you want, but wanting what you have."** Most people look at happiness exactly opposite of Shakespeare's idea of happiness. They look around and notice what they do not have; and become depressed.

If you get your eyes off the "greenness" of your neighbor's grass, you can appreciate your grass more. If anything, you should use the inspiration of your neighbor's example to improve your situation! Go out and get some fertilizer and work on your grass. Buy some more grass seeds. Water your grass daily. Then you will discover that your neighbor's green grass was available to you all along. Of course, I am over-simplifying this. There are some things that your neighbor may have that you may never afford. But happiness, as you should know by now, cannot be bought with money. If so, you would never see an unhappy rich person.

When someone else appears to have a wonderful life, it may not be as glorious as you think. I know a lady who looked at a married man and said, "If that man ever divorces, he will be mine! I bet I know how to satisfy him!" Well, within two years the man got a divorce. This same lady, whom I will call Mary, began dating the man, whom I will call Harry. After six months, Mary and Harry were married. Harry was Mary's dream come true. Things went well until about three months later.

The phone rang. I picked it up , and Mary was on the other end. "This lying hypocrite," she began "is nothing but a self-centered, egotistical bast_rd!" I interrupted,

"Calm down, and take your time." She understood my message and said, "Oh, I'm sorry. Please excuse my language, but that man really knows how to tick me off." She continued, "I guess you can tell there is big trouble in paradise. It has only been three months, and Harry treats me like I'm a piece of trash. I see why his ex-wife couldn't live with him." With tears in her voice, she continued, "I'm a human being, just like he is. I have feelings, too!" Mary had just discovered that her new husband was an old philanderer.

Immediately I reflected on the occasion when Mary said, "If that man ever divorces, he will be mine." Well, now, Harry was all hers and she could not stand him. She wanted out of the marriage. When she was on the outside looking in, Harry was the best looking, best dressed man she had ever seen. He drove a nice car and lived in a nice home. But once Mary had Harry, she discovered that he was up to his limit on all his credit cards. He had a huge home equity loan. He had child support payments. He even had an immense, delinquent hospital bill. Besides this, she discovered he owed over $2,000 to the Internal Revenue Service. When Mary saw the complete picture of Harry, she discovered that what she thought to be "green grass" was actually brown! Mary learned, rather quickly, that "all that glitters is not gold."

Most people, like children, see something they like and want it. I notice, especially during the Christmas season, that whenever my children see a commercial for a toy or doll, they holler, "I want that." They are totally content, until they see something they do not already have. Regardless of how much we have, there is something about human nature that cries out for something new, something bigger, something better. There is an insatiable appetite in man for things and achievement. We never get enough. We never accomplish enough. **What we see is what we want.** So to be happy, we must learn to set limits for ourselves. Otherwise, we will over extend ourselves in debt, time and energy. You see, after the thrill of the hunt, you need to be able to sit down and enjoy today's catch, without worrying about tomorrow's. So what if someone has a bigger catch than you? At least you are not hungry. You have enough to be content.

If you spend your time comparing your life to others who have more, you'll make your life miserable. My philosophy is very simple: **1) Don't compare; 2) don't compete and 3) don't complain.** Just these three simple suggestions can help you avert a lot of disappointment and discouragement. They can even help to alleviate a lot of stress from your life. And best of all, in my opinion, they will tremendously improve your general attitude in life! The truth is that you do not have to "keep up with the Jones'." Let the Jones' be the Jones', and you be content in uniquely being the Smiths.

When you think about it, what we really like about the Jones' is the image they portray. It does not matter what we are. What matters to us is what others think we are. When it all boils down, we are more interested in images than reality. When companies advertise, they do not advertise a product. They advertise an image. Advertisers know that if they can sell us on the image, we will automatically go out and buy the product that will give us that image. That philosophy is simple: **What you see is what you want.**

So how do we get a grip on ourselves with the myriad of visual images that bombards us every day? Do we have to yield every time an image of something whets our appetites? **You can make a covenant with your eyes!** The biblical character, Job, made a covenant with his eyes.

I made a covenant with mine eyes; why then should I think upon a maid?

Job 31:1

Do you realize that you can make covenants with parts of your body? You will actually be surprised how successful you can be if you only learn to make a deal or covenant with yourself. Let us say you have a genuine weakness for chocolate. So someone bets you $100 that you cannot go a week without chocolate. Under those circumstances, I believe you could do it because you will have made a bet or covenant to do it! The point is that **we never do any more than we are committed to do in our hearts.** Yet, it remains that God cannot bless us beyond the level of our commitment! Of course, every time we make a commitment, we must make some sacrifices in order to keep those commitments. But **the greater the sacrifice, the greater the blessing!**

Job made a covenant with his eyes not to lust. To do that, however, required that he censor everything to which he exposed himself. Thus, when we make a covenant with our eyes, that means we must censor our movies, television programs, live shows, books and magazines, videos and even the association of who we choose to be our friends. What you see will not only affect an emotional response in you, but it will affect the way you think. When your thinking is affected, your actions are affected. Therefore, the best thing is to guard yourself to what you are exposed. To put it in a more proverbial form, **"Out of sight, out of mind."**

You may be content to sit in a room and look at television. When all of a sudden, someone comes in with some cookies or potato chips or fried chicken. Now you feel compelled to have some because you saw it. Just seeing it brought the desire to your mind. Ever notice that the very first sin was a sin of the **eyes?**

And when the woman saw that the tree was good for food, and that it was pleasant to the eyes, and a tree to be desired to make one wise, she took of the fruit thereof, and did eat, and gave also unto her husband with her; and he did eat. And the eyes of them both were opened, and they knew that they were naked; and they sewed fig leaves together, and made themselves aprons.
Genesis 3:6-7

Interestingly, the fruit caught their **eyes**, but it opened up their **minds!** The lesson we learn from this is to keep our eyes off forbidden fruit.

Intimate fellowship with those whose lifestyles are contrary to biblical teaching are a part of forbidden fruit for Christians. Remember, **"Association brings about assimilation."**

I wrote you in my [previous] letter not to associate (closely and habitually) with unchaste (impure) people; Not [meaning, of course, that you must] altogether shun the immoral people of this world, or the greedy graspers and cheats and thieves or idolaters, since otherwise you would need to get out of the world and human society altogether! But now I write to you not to associate with any one who bears the name of [Christian] brother, if he is known to be guilty of immorality or greed, or is an idolater — that is, whose soul is devoted to any object that usurps the place of God — or [is] a person with a foul tongue (railing, abusing, reviling, slandering), or is a drunkard, or a swindler or a robber. [No] you must not so much as eat with such a person.

I Corinthians 5:9-11 AMP

Do you understand why it is so detrimental to get intimately involved with immoral people? Because **sin is contagious.** Just listening to sinful lifestyles will sound fun and adventurous. Their irreverence will soon rub off on you. Then you will be prone to having fantasies. And that is where sin begins — in fantasy and imagination. **Do not go around temptation to try to prove how strong you are because you will only discover how weak you are!**

Remember Eve kept hanging around the forbidden fruit. The more she looked, the more she desired. It is the same way with pornography. The more you see, the more you will want to see. But eventually you will want to touch and become involved with more serious things. So you see, Eve really broke God's covenant with her eyes, not with her mouth! Then, as a result, when Adam and Eve broke their covenant with God, they lost "God-consciousness" and gained "self-consciousness."

If we really want to keep certain things out of our

mind, we must also make a covenant with our mouths
and our ears. You see, you can speak certain things and
bring up images in your mind. Or, you can passively listen to certain things and create mental images. For that
matter, you can even touch or smell or taste things that
will immediately create images in your mind. So all of
our five senses can stimulate thoughts in the mind. One
woman told me, "If I just smell bread baking, I have to
have something, made with bread, to eat!" Another
woman confessed, "Every time I smell a man's cologne,
my hormones get all worked up!" One man admitted,
"If I go a long time without sex, the touch of a woman's
arm gets me sexually aroused." So you see, all of your
senses can cause certain images to come to your mind. I
remember recently making a phone call to place an order
for some supplies. When right in the middle of my
order, the customer service representative remarked,
"Your voice is so smooth and sexy that I can feel a warm
sensation going over my body."

Here again, one of the physical senses was making an
impact on the mind. The mind, in turn, makes an impact
on the body. Spoken words affect the mind, because
words create images. For example, without seeing my
car, I could use words to describe it and give you a mental picture of it. Never underestimate the power of
words that you speak or hear! Words persuade or dis-
suade. What we see, then, only becomes a visual aid to
words. "Show and tell" is the most powerful combination we have in the art of communication.

Not only do our physical senses have a direct impact
on our minds, but our minds have a direct impact on our

senses. Therefore, we must guard our environment. We must abide in a controlled atmosphere. If not, we begin to die just like a fish taken out of water. We have to make a covenant with our eyes in order to guard our thought life.

The light of the body is the eye: therefore, when thine eye is single, thy whole body also is full of light; but when thine eye is evil, thy body also is full of darkness.
Luke 11:34

More than anything else, the eyes readily tell about the condition of the body. The minute a person becomes intoxicated or "high," the eyes will become blood shot, red or glazed. If our bodies are not well, a doctor can generally detect it by merely looking into our eyes. The eyes tell a lot, both naturally and spiritually.

Whether or not you know, the eyes do a lot of talking. You can send loud and clear signals across the room with your eyes. With your eyes you can say, "I hate you." With your eyes you can say, "I am jealous of you." With your eyes you can say, "I love you." Even with your eyes you can say, "I want to flirt with you." Years ago, parents would use their eyes to discipline their children. Mama could simply look at her child and send the message, "Sit down and be still or else I will give you a whipping you will never forget!"

There is communicative power in your eyes. Use it constructively. Use it to make a covenant so that you do not lose control of your desires. Use that power to control your greed. Use it to keep your appetites in check. Do you have a problem with impulse buying? Make a serious covenant with your eyes that you will only purchase what you need when you can afford it. Many lives are in over-indulgence because individuals do not make covenants with their eyes! Are you tempted to want to taste everything that looks good which passes before you? Make a covenant with your eyes that you will only eat **your** lunch, nothing else. You do not have to allow what you see to be your master. You are in total control of what you eat, what you buy and whom you are committed to in relationships. Make a covenant with your eyes that instead of "having what you want," you will begin appreciating and wanting what you already have.

So the next time you are tempted by something you see, speak to yourself and make a covenant. When you see a new car that appeals to you, make a covenant and say, "I cannot afford another car right now, but I am glad to have the one I have. It suits my purposes." When you are tempted to stop at a fast food restaurant, make a covenant by saying, "Sure it would be easier to eat out, but I have plenty of food at home that I can warm up. My food is even more wholesome!" When you are tempted by someone's physical attractiveness, make a covenant. You can say, "I am already in a rewarding relationship with someone who loves me dearly. I will not risk my relationship to chase vanity and wind up disappointed." There is always a down side to every temptation. There is a high price to pay for low living! So before you leap into a situation, look very carefully. Take your time to investigate it and count the cost! Make time to make a covenant with your eyes so your emotions will not make a decision apart from your spirit. **If "what you see is what you want," then you had**

better make sure that you are seeing the right thing at the right time! Making a covenant with your eyes is not so much for God's sake, but for yours. Make a covenant today and respect it as though you had made a thousand dollar bet to insure it. If you give your covenant the proper value, you will fulfill it!

Your covenant is like a target you personally establish. You must have a target in order to hit one. When I was younger, I remember having trouble shooting the moving target in an arcade game. I have always had a steady hand and vision with the perspicacity of an eagle. Yet, whenever I would position myself, take careful aim and fire, I would miss the target! I know that my aim was on target, but I continued to miss. After a series of repeating the same mistake, it occurred to me exactly what I was doing wrong. I was aiming at the target, when I should have been aiming ahead of the target.

I had to learn to anticipate where the target was going. I had to estimate the speed of the target and plan my shot accordingly. You see, the key to hitting the target is not based on where the target is, but where it is going. This means that if you are going to hit a certain target or reach a particular goal, you must plan ahead. **A lack of adequate preparation is the reason for every failure!**

Most young people do not attain high goals or long term goals at an early age because they constantly aim **at** the moving target instead of planning a strategy to hit where it is moving. Big businesses understand this principle and use extrapolation to plan for changes in the marketplace. But many young people are victims of instant gratification. Their behavior is motivated by what seems good at the time. Irresponsibility, recklessness and aberrant lifestyles are the results of spontaneity. We cannot live in a "perpetual now" and expect to be successful down the road. When a young person commits a heinous crime of violence, he is not considering the harsh reality of the consequences of his actions. He simply acts impulsively to vent his anger, frustration and stress. This is shooting at the target rather than aiming a little in front of the target.

Plain and simple, success requires a plan. **If you do not have a plan to succeed, by default you have a plan for failure!** There is no need to worry about where you are, concentrate on where you are going! And with a planned strategy coupled with a little patience and diligence, you will get there.

CHAPTER 3
Taming The Dog

"But, in spite of how much love you think people have, there is still a little dog in every man and a little witch in every woman!"

I shall never forget a particular preaching engagement in a quaint country town in Georgia. Immediately after delivering a sermon about love, I was accosted by a gray haired woman. She came up to me and candidly said, "Baby, everything you said was fine and sweet. But, in spite of how much love you think people have, **there is still a little dog in every man and a little witch in every woman!**" She then patted the top of my hand, told me, "God bless you," and walked out of the church. At the time I had no clue about the meaning of this woman's words. But shortly thereafter, I read something that Apostle Paul said:

We know that the Law is spiritual; but I am a creature of the flesh (carnal, unspiritual), having been sold into slavery under [the control of] sin. For I do not understand my own actions — I am baffled, bewildered. I do not practice or accomplish what I wish, but I do the very thing that I loathe [which my moral instinct condemns]. Now if I do [habitually] what is contrary to my desire, [that means that] I acknowledge and agree that the Law is good (morally excellent) and that I take sides with it. However, it is no longer I who do the deed, but the sin [principle] which is at home in me and has possession of me. For I know that nothing good dwells within me, that is, in my flesh. I can will what is right, but I cannot perform it. — I have the intention and urge to do what is right, but no power to carry it out; For I fail to practice the good deeds I desire to do, but the evil deeds that I do not desire to do are what I am [ever] doing. Now if I do what I do not desire to do, it is no longer I doing it — it is not myself that acts — but the sin [prin-

ciple] which dwells within me [fixed and operating in my soul]. So I find it to be a law [of my being] that when I want to do what is right and good, evil is ever present with me and I am subject to its insistent demands. For I endorse and delight in the Law of God in my inmost self — with my new nature. But I discern in my bodily members — in the sensitive appetites and wills of the flesh — a different law (rule of action) at war against the law of my mind (my reason) and making me a prisoner to the law of sin that dwells in my bodily organs — in the sensitive appetites and wills of the flesh.
Romans 7:14-23 AMP

In spite of Paul's spirituality, he had problems taming the dog within. There was always something on the inside that wanted to do wrong. As you know, this inner conflict is not peculiar to Paul. We all struggle with a dual nature of good and evil. Sometimes we feel that there is an angel on one shoulder encouraging us to do right, and a devil on the other shoulder trying to persuade us to do wrong. This dichotomy sometimes spins us into such confusion that we make an impulsive decision. So what can we do to abate this internal war?

Regardless of our degree of holiness, there will still be a "bad dog" in us. No matter how much we read the Bible, that dog will remain faithfully within us. Despite the fervency of our prayer life, that dog will not abandon us. That unregenerate nature within will say, "Do unto others **before** they do unto you." That unredeemed nature will say, "An eye for an eye and a tooth for a tooth." That low down dog nature will mockingly say, "Ah ha. That's what you get! I told you so." That nature will even suggest to you, "Lay your religion down, and tell her off." This same "dog nature" makes you want to retort evil for evil. So how do we get rid of this "bad dog"? **We do not get rid of the "bad dog." We simply tame him!**

Every time you have an opportunity to do right, evil will be present to discourage you. So to help us better focus on the voice that encourages good, we have to learn to tune out the voice of discouragement. Of course, when you tune out something, that does not mean it no longer exists. It only means you are no longer sensitive to it. So it can be there, but you will not be conscious of it.

When I first moved out of my parents' home, I moved to a location which was not very far from an airport. For the first few days I recall consciously taking note of the number of airplanes flying overhead. However within the first week, I no longer heard the noise of planes flying. Had the planes ceased flying? No, in fact, the traffic at the airport grew and additional runways were added. I simply grew immune to the noise of the planes. As far as I was concerned, they no longer existed. Every now and then, when I would think about an airplane, I could hear the vibrations of a powerful jet engine. Those big jets could make a lot of noise, but they had no right to land on my property.

The bad dog within is just like those airplanes. He will do a lot of barking (make a lot of noise), but he has no authority to land in your space. Just tune out the barking of the dog by concentrating on other things. Quote some scriptures and drown out the dog's bark/voice.

Before we had separate alarm clocks, my wife and I shared the same one. I would set the clock each night to alarm at 6:00 a.m. in the morning. When 6:00 a.m. arrived, I would always turn off the alarm and get up. Sometimes I would have to shake my wife to make sure she was awake because most of the time she did not hear the alarm sound. The reason she would not hear the alarm was because she had become accustomed to me hearing and responding to the alarm. She was conditioned to ignore the alarm because she knew I would turn it off. Likewise, when each of our children was in infancy, my wife would get up in the night and tend to their needs. There were many, many times when I never heard the baby crying in the night, but my wife did.

I was always sensitive to hearing the alarm clock because I was the one who had to quickly respond to cut it off. On the other hand, my wife was always sensitive to hearing the baby because she was the one who had to get up, breast feed and change the baby. So here is the point: **You will always be sensitive to whatever you respond.** If you are responsible for a certain area, you will always be sensitive to that area. Now, if you want to decrease your sensitivity to the bad dog's voice, you must stop responding to what he suggests to you. When the dog within tries to infuriate you, ignore him. Pay no attention to him when he tries to scare you. He is all bark and no bite. He just wants to scare and discourage you into hurting yourself.

Paul, writing to the Church at Philippi, said, *"Beware of dogs" (Phil. 3:2).* "Beware" means "to be aware" of something. Although the word "dog" is used literally in many places of Scripture, it is used metaphorically of those who are full of deception, false teaching and/or moral impurity. So if you are going to be effective in conquering your "dog nature," you must first know what your dog nature is.

To some, the inner "dog" they must be aware of is an irrepressible sex nature. To others it may be a struggle with bisexuality or homosexuality. The dog for someone else may be a weakness for pornography. The dog in others is an uncontrolled appetite for food. Another dog is an unrestrained craving for drugs or alcohol. Some dogs are itching ears that love to hear slander. Some are burning tongues that love to spread gossip. Some dogs are passive natures which struggle with pride. Some are dogs of cowardice and timidity. Some are quick tempers and foul mouths. Some dogs are even rationalizing minds that love to bring intellectual justification for immoral behavior!

Despite what your "dog" is, you need to be aware of it! By now you should know that the first step to treatment is the acknowledgment of the problem. Remember, **you cannot conquer what you will not confront!** Know your enemies! An older man once told me, "It is better to know where your enemies stand, than to know where your friends sit." The whole idea here is that the better you know your enemy, the better you know his weaknesses. The better you know your enemy, the better you know how to attack, defeat and subdue him! The better you know your enemy, the better you know how to defend yourself against his attacks.

I have heard some Christians argue, "Jesus defeated the devil. He plundered Satan's kingdom and took the keys of hell and death. Now we have the victory!" Yes, Jesus defeated the devil! Hallelujah for that! Yes, Jesus took the keys of hell and death! Praise the Lord! But you and I will still have problems with the devil. Do you know why? **Because although Satan was defeated, he has not yet been destroyed!** Likewise, you can and will defeat your "dog nature" many times, but you will not destroy it. Thus, you will have trial after trial with your dog nature.

Since the dog nature will not be destroyed until the flesh sees corruption, you and I must learn to subdue it. We must put our dog on a leash. **Stop letting the "dog" run loose; put him on a leash!** Then whenever he tries to lead us out of bounds, all we have to do is firmly yank the leash. Use a Bible verse to pull him back in line. Verse by verse, we build a chain which we simply slip around the dog's neck. Consequently, whenever you want to put pressure on the dog, quote a verse. Putting the Word of God on the devil always chokes him.

The most ferocious dog can be tamed. The most hyperactive dog can be subdued. The most iconoclastic dog can be trained. The most obstinate and insubordinate dog can be made into an obedient one. You see, the flesh, without the spirit of God, is mere animal. If we do not have a personal relationship with Christ, we are like dogs without a conscience. A dog has no remorse, regret or repentance. A dog is ruled by his nature. His nature is naturally dirty. He will drink out of toilets. He will eat out of a trash can or off the floor. Sometimes he will even consume his own vomit and feces. That is just a part of a dog's nature.

On the other hand, the spirit of God brings a certain kind of refinement to our lives. It tames the dog nature little by little. The spirit of God operating in our lives begins to clean up our drinking habits. He begins to change the desires for the things to which we expose ourselves. The Holy Spirit helps us to tame the dog in us. A new nature is formed in us that gradually changes our old nature.

The indwelling presence of the Holy Spirit changes the nature of our spirits. Then our new spirits change the nature of our minds. Finally, our new minds change the nature of our bodies or fleshly natures. Although the Holy Spirit is within us, sporadically we may still have ungodly desires to pop up in our mind or body. Of course, that does not mean you are out of fellowship with God. It simply means that a temptation to sin is being presented to your mind or body. But remember that **being tempted is not a sin. Only yielding to the temptation is sin.** You see, Jesus was tempted to sin, but He never yielded. It's true, we cannot control what temptation comes to us, however, you can control what temptation dwells with you.

How do you keep a temptation from dwelling with you? You must change what you are thinking. Remember, your spirit is the only part of you that is ever redeemed. Your mind has not been redeemed yet, neither has your body. Therefore, you must take the initiative to do something about your unredeemed mind. Otherwise, it will continue to bring you thoughts of corruption and sin which are in rebellion to God's will.

Do not be conformed to this world — this age, fashioned after and adapted to its external, superficial customs. But be transformed (changed) by the [entire] renewal of your mind — by its new ideals and its new attitude — so that you may prove [for yourselves] what is the good and acceptable and perfect will of God, even the thing which is good and acceptable and perfect [in His sight for you].

Romans 12:2 AMP

I always suggest renewing the mind with the Word of God. I do not know of anything that has as much life, truth and power as the Bible.

For the Word that God speaks is alive and full of power — making it active, operative, energizing and effective; it is sharper than any two-edged sword, penetrating to the dividing line of the breath of life (soul) and [the immortal] spirit, and of joints and marrow [that is, of the deepest parts of our nature] exposing and sifting and analyzing and judging the very thoughts and purposes of the heart.

Hebrews 4:12 AMP

The Word of God is life changing. It is a dynamic book that is much, much more than a literary masterpiece. The Word of God will change your thinking, your attitude, your actions and hence, your circumstances! It is of utmost importance that we spend quality time basking in the precious truths of the Bible.

For our most comprehensive change, we must do something with our spirits, minds and bodies. Many people develop their minds or bodies at the expense of their spirits. But we are tripartite beings, so we need to have a balance. I have seen several intellectuals try to relate to God only with their minds. They do not involve their spirit or emotions. They methodically serve God via various religious traditions. They employ good deeds as a mental catharsis. That is, their pious service acts as a mental purgative to disseminate guilt. **The fact remains that God is a spirit!** And if we are going to relate to Him, we must relate to Him spiritually *(John 4:24)*.

Over-development of the body inhibits some from balancing the development of their spirit and mind. Some people can spend hours a day working out in the gym. Yet they spend little or no time developing their minds or spirits. Regardless of how you view it, that is off-balance. Priorities are severely misconstrued when we can give hours of attention to the care of the body, but neglect the spirit. Think about it. Think about the amount of time spent jogging, walking or doing aerobics. Think about the time spent on our hair, in salons or barber shops. Think about the time spent on our nails. Think about the time spent shopping for clothes for our bodies. Think about the time spent feeding the body. Please do not get me wrong, these things are needful, but we should not neglect the intangible aspects of our mind and spirit. There should be a balance among these.

We must learn to apportion our time so that we develop our spirits, educate our minds and train our bodies. I believe we should always work from the inside outwardly. The spirit, you see, is the framework for the body. The internal framework supports the external structure. So if you really want the structure to be sturdy and durable, you need to give special attention to the foundation and framework. That is the spiritual part of you.

Most people who are unkempt are so because their spiritual life is unkempt. So if you want to tame and groom the dog nature, you must first discipline your spirit.

For God did not give us a spirit of timidity — of cowardice, of craven and cringing and fawning fear — but [He has given us a spirit] of power and of love and of calm and well-balanced mind and discipline and self-control.

II Timothy 1:7 AMP

Do you realize that God has given you the spirit of a disciplined mind? You may not be using your gift of discipline, but that does not negate the fact that God gave it to you. That is an inestimable gift. Evidently, young Timothy was not using his gift. Before Paul talked about having a spirit of a disciplined mind, he admonished Timothy to *"stir up the gift of God..."* (*II Timothy 1:6).* Whether or not you know it, there is discipline within you. You simply have to stir it up. Just start using it. Determine that, as of this moment, you are going to exercise your flabby muscles of discipline. Then the more you exercise them, the stronger they will become. Soon you will be super spiritually fit, mentally fit and physically fit. A disciplined mind will even help you to be financially and emotionally fit.

With a disciplined mind, you can control yourself and your dog nature. **The wonderful thing about a dog**

is that he can be trained! He can be trained to attack or to protect. He can be trained to fetch or to stay. He can be trained to bark or to be quiet. But he can be trained. Once you have trained your "dog," he can become a faithful friend to you instead of your greatest enemy. Despite the adage "You can't teach an old dog new tricks," I believe you can. You simply have to stir up the teachable nature in the dog. **But no matter how old, a dog can be trained!**

CHAPTER 4
Just Do It

"You cannot sit around and carefully plan every step of your life and anticipate the results. Sometimes you just have to do it! If you think about some things too long, you will talk yourself out of them."

A girl held on to the back of my bicycle to insure that I would not fall. She followed me up and down the street. Suddenly, as I rapidly coasted down the street, I turned around and noticed that the girl had let go of my bike. There she was, waving down the street at me, and I was thinking, "Who is holding up my bike now?" Then it dawned on me that I was riding on my own. This girl taught me how to ride a bike! But I did not know I could ride a bike until she turned me loose!

You cannot sit around and carefully plan every step of your life and anticipate the results. Sometimes you just have to do it! If you think about some things too long, you will talk yourself out of them. Fear will over-take you. You see, **you must be willing to lose before you are ready to gain.** When you are convinced that there is something that you should be doing, do it! Do not wait around for the perfect opportunity. Just do it! Follow the faith in your heart, not the fear and doubt in your head!

When you think about it, what do you really have to lose? I do not know about you, but I would rather try to succeed and fail than fail without trying. Most people want the best in life, but they are too afraid to risk what is mediocre in order to get what is best. In other words, we like the sweet things in life. We like the honey, but we are afraid of the bees that we must confront to get the honey. We allow the potential penalty, which is in the stinger of the bee, to keep us away from the reward of the sweetness of the honey. You see, if you focus on the stinger, fear will come. And that fear will keep you away from the honey. But if you focus on the honey, motivation will come. And that motivation will move you towards the honey.

So when you want a little sweetness in life, forget about the stinger. Think about the honey and just go for it! Just do it! Most people who are super successful had a haunch about something and followed that haunch. They had no guarantees. All they had to go on was a haunch, an instinct, an intuition. If they thought about the stinger, they would have no honey. That is, they would have no money! After you have tossed an idea around and you feel good about it, move on it or someone else will! After you have prayed about it and you discern that it is in God's will for you, go for it! After you have talked about it and talked about it and talked about it, do it!

That reminds me of Bishop Wright of the Evangelical United Brethren Church, who did not believe man could fly or should fly. During one of his revivals in the midwestern states, he made the bold statement, "If God had meant for man to fly, He would have given him wings!" Meanwhile, his own sons, Wilbur and Orville Wright, were back home in North Carolina developing the first successful airplane! Yes, Bishop Wright's sons, the Wright Brothers, had a haunch that man could fly. They believed that haunch, although they had never seen it done. But those brothers were born to teach men to fly. In fact, since aviation was their only passion, the Wright Brothers both died as bachelors.

Whether or not you know it, there is a bird within you that is ready to soar. But you are the one who is responsible for pushing that bird out of his nest. As long as a bird has something underneath him, he will not fly. You have to launch out into unsupported territory in order to discover you can fly. Before I discovered I could ride a bicycle, the girl had to turn me loose. When you are loosed, you either fly or die. You either do it and fly and enjoy the thrill of the flight, or you sit back and die with unfulfilled dreams!

You may attempt some things and fail, but at least you made an effort. There is a thrilling reward, just for making the effort. You may get tired, but God will help you.

He [God] giveth power to the faint; and to them that have no might he increaseth strength. Even the youths shall faint and be weary, and the young men shall utterly fall: But they that wait upon the Lord shall renew their strength; they shall mount up with wings as eagles; they shall run, and not be weary; and they shall walk, and not faint.

Isaiah 40:29-31

If you want to fly, you have to take on the nature of an eagle. You have to change your thinking. Just because you have not flown, does not mean you cannot fly! An eagle knows he can fly, but what about you? If you are not careful you can have the nature of a pigeon. Although pigeons can fly, you normally see them on downtown sidewalks and the outskirts of buildings. Pigeons can fly, but when we see them, they are walking. For years I have noticed that pigeons do an awful lot of walking. It sometimes takes the scare of a gunshot to make a pigeon fly. And even then, it will only fly off and make a large circle. Then the pigeon will come back to the same place or vicinity it was initially located. Pigeons act like acrophobic creatures. They live beneath their privilege. Pigeons are nice birds, but they do not go anywhere. They make no real progress. Does that sound like someone you know?

By contrast, an eagle is a peculiar bird. He does not travel in flocks. Eagles are more independent. Eagles are like leaders, you only find them one by one, not in groups. Unlike vultures and buzzards, eagles subsist mainly on live prey and are monogamous in their mating relationships. If you ever scrutinize the mannerisms of an eagle, you will scarcely see an eagle flap its wings more than a few flaps until it can find an updraft. Once an eagle finds a thermal column of air, he will relax and lock his wings into a full spread. Then he circles and circles in that upward moving column of air, gaining altitude with each 360 degree revolution. We learn from the eagle that we cannot fight the air, if we are going to fly. We must flow with it. We sometimes spend much of our time struggling with circumstances instead of "waiting upon the Lord." We have to learn to simply find a warm column of air (or should I say prayer?) and spread our wings of faith and relax.

One of the keys to doing your best is in your ability to relax. When you see a professional in action, he always appears relaxed. He makes a very difficult feat seem smooth and easy. So after we find the right column of warm air, we should just circle upward. Remember, warm air always rises. That tells you that you need to associate yourself with people who are upwardly mobile. Spend time in circles of people who talk up and look up and think up!

In another sense, I honestly believe the circling in the column of warm air has significance to consistency and faithfulness. For example, every year, I read through the Bible. That is a form of circling for me. But each time I circle through the Scripture, I find myself being elevated. I get a higher understanding of certain things. I circle through a routine of daily prayer, and every round goes higher and higher. As we circle, we do the same things God tells us to do over and over. We continue doing those things until we are lifted to where He wants us to be. As we serve God through our consistency, faithfulness and loyalty, God rewards us by exalting or promoting us.

So our primary responsibility is to find the right column of warm air, set our wings and relax. There is no need for us to make a lot of commotion by just flapping our wings. We flap them just enough to find the upward flow of the Holy Spirit, and relax. You know, too much flapping can not only slow you down, but tire you out! I believe that when you do too much flapping, you are trying to rise to great heights on your own merits instead of trusting the updrafts of warm air into the heavens. Think of it this way, the **Holy Spirit is the wind beneath our wings!** He gets under us as we stretch out on Him. He lifts us up! We do not fly and reach great heights by flapping against His will, but by cooperating with His flow.

All we need to do is to find the right current and spread our wings. The rest is left up to God-ordained laws of gravity and aerodynamics of which we have nothing to do. We simply cooperate with those laws to produce a particular, desired effect. God controls the laws. We control our obedience to the laws.

Unfortunately, some people will never reach the heights of the eagle because they will not cooperate with the laws that will take them to those heights. Others will never reach the eagle's height because they have a sparrow's mentality. You see, you can never get a sparrow to fly at an altitude of 10,000 feet. Sparrows are low flying birds. They are more interested in insects on the ground than in updrafts into the heavens. If we are not careful, we can develop a sparrow's mentality, always looking for insects. A sparrow mentality looks for pettiness. It looks for flaws. It looks for something negative about which to talk.

When you are on your way up like an eagle, you need to continue to look up! For some strange reason, I notice that we tend to move in the direction that we are looking. If we are looking down, our life tends to experience a magnified amount of negative happenings. Likewise, when we are looking up, we take note of every positive thing that is happening to us. As a result, more positive things happen. People are drawn to be around positive, successful people. So set your mind, heart and affections on things that are above and not beneath!

Remember that we are risen with Christ, and He is concerned about things which are above. In fact we are challenged with, *"If ye then be risen with Christ, seek those things which are above, where Christ sitteth on the right hand of God. Set your affection on things above, not on things on the earth" (Col. 3:1-2).* Understand that **we are not called to be victims of the circumstances, but victors over the circumstances.**

Where do you abide— under the circumstances or over them? Do you allow things or people to get you down, or do you get over them by "mounting with wings as an eagle"? If you are down, you need to spread your wings and find where the new winds of the Holy Spirit are blowing. That might mean forsaking dead traditions and meaningless rituals to feed on things that are full of life as the eagles do.

When you begin feeding on things that are full of life, your strength becomes renewed. Then when you mount up with wings as eagles, you see the world, and life in general, from an entirely new vantage point. It is only natural that when you get above circumstances, you see a more balanced picture of what is going on. What a beautiful view to see things from above! The world is absolutely beautiful from an aerial perspective. Whenever you look at things from above, you never see a lot of dirt and imperfections. Everything looks neat and even. The geometric shapes appear flawless. The colors are gorgeously balanced. Everything seems like a carefully grafted puzzle, comfortably put together.

If things do not look good from your present position, you need to change positions. You need to get airborne so you can see things as the eagle. Then you can swoop down and take your prey by surprise. Wherever you are in life, there is always room to rise!

And the Lord shall make thee the head, and not the tail; and thou shalt be above only, and thou shalt not be beneath; if that thou hearken unto the commandments of the Lord thy God, which I command thee this day, to observe and to do them.

Deuteronomy 28:13

Can you see that wonderful promise from the Lord? If you are consistent, faithful and loyal to the Lord and His Word, you are in line for a promotion. When you honor God, He will lift you up!

Do not forget to do your part. First, you must be consistent. That is, you must exhibit a stability in your character that is not fickle. An honest person, for example, must consistently be honest. He cannot be honest only on Tuesdays and Thursdays. If you are an honest person, that character trait will follow you always. You are consistently honest, not just partly honest.

Secondly, you must be faithful. If you are hired for a job that requires you to report to work at 9:00 a.m., you should be there, faithfully, by 9:00 a.m. A faithful employee will not drag in late several mornings. A faithful employee will be there every day, on time! A faithful person is a dependable person. However, there is a difference between being faithful and being consistent. A certain young man, with whom I am acquainted, knows how to be extremely faithful. His only problem is that he is not consistently faithful. He may be unusually faithful for three months. Then you will not see him for a while. He is a faithful man, but he is not consistent. He is even totally faithful in some areas, but completely unpredictable in other areas. He is sporadically faithful, so that makes him inconsistent.

The third character trait we need to possess in order to be lifted up is loyalty. Loyalty is considerably differ-

ent from faithfulness. You see, an employee may faithfully show up for work at 9:00 a.m. However, he may
steal things from his job. He may cheat on the job. He
may goof off and steal company time. He can be faithful without being loyal. I know some men who faithfully provide for their families, yet they are not loyal to
their wives.

So if you intend to be "the head and not the tail,
above only and not beneath," you are going to have to
demonstrate consistency, faithfulness and loyalty to God
and His commands. You see, I frankly do not believe
God will bless mess! I do not think God will exalt
inconsistency, unfaithfulness or disloyalty. To do that
would send the wrong message to people. It would actually be as though God were endorsing bad character.

But God endorses and rewards faithfulness and obedience. Before God will promote, He will make sure we
have been faithful over the little. Then He rewards our
obedience. You know, if a leader does not know how to
receive instructions, he is not qualified to give instructions. Yet, if a person knows how to submit and obey the
Word of the Lord, God brings blessings in their life.

Remember what God told Joshua as he was assuming
leadership from Moses?

*This book of the law shall not depart out of thy
mouth; but thou shalt meditate therein day and night,
that thou mayest observe to do according to all that is
written therein: for then thou shalt make thy way pros-
perous, and then thou shalt have good success.*
                    Joshua 1:8

The main reason we have the Word of God is to **do**

what the Word says. The Lord is much more interested in our walking the walk, than talking the talk. God is telling us to meditate on the Word and **just do it!** If it is the Word of God, you do not even have to think twice about it. **Just do it!**

When you have something that you dread doing, do not keep procrastinating. **Just do it!** There are many things we know which have to be done. Yet we sit back and talk about how hard it is going to be and how long it will take. Doing that only makes it harder to get started. You see, when you dreadfully approach something that must be done, you make that job harder. So when you have something to do that is unpleasant, **just do it.** Go ahead and get through with it.

When I was growing up, my father would make me eat certain health food concoctions that were disgusting to my taste buds. Yet I knew that I had to consume them. So I would hold my nose and gulp them down. The unpleasant feeling and taste did not last very long. I just did what I had to do.

Whenever you put off what you have to do, it causes your mountain or problem to grow. As more time elapses, the problem gets bigger and harder to approach. You will also discover that tackling the big problems will not seem as problematic as you would have made them to be in your mind. If you have to go to the doctor to get a shot, just go on and get it and be through with it! There is no need to waste your time squirming, crying and dreading the whole experience. Just do what you have to do and what you need to do and get through with it! I mean, when the alarm clock sounds early in the morning, it serves no worthwhile purpose to lie in bed and dread getting up. You know you have to get up, so **just do it!**

CHAPTER 5
Sticking To It

"The right frame of mind will give you the right attitude about what you intend to do."

There are two challenging aspects of doing a job. The first is getting started. The second is getting finished. It is very easy to relegate things to the future. We often do this because we do not want to expend the necessary time and energy to accomplish the job. So we end up procrastinating. Actually, before you get started, you need to be in the right frame of mind. The right frame of mind will give you the right attitude about what you intend to do. Then, once your attitude about the job is right, you can approach the situation with excitement and anticipation.

A few months ago, I went into my study/library at home. I looked on my desk and paper was everywhere. Books were there. Mail was stacked high. Tax information was there. Check stubs were scattered about. Computer disks were in various places. Magazines were spread around. A couple of my Bibles lay to the side. My entire desk looked like a war zone. I kept saying to myself, "I am going to come in here and clean up my desk tomorrow." Then on Fridays I would say, "I am going to come in here and clean my desk next week." I was at the point where I felt discombobulated every time I looked at my disheveled desk.

The disorganization of my desk befuddled my frame of mind. I could not concentrate well with my desk in that condition. So if something was to be done, I had to take the initiative to do it! The first thing I did was to change my frame of mind. I had to make a determination to clear the clutter on my desk. In changing the frame of my mind, I had to give value to clearing my desk. So I thought to myself, "If I clean my desk, my thoughts will be clearer. I will be able to get more done in less time because of an organized atmosphere."

Immediately after giving value to clearing the clutter from my desk, my mind was in the right frame to start the job and finish the job. You see, the things that are done with priority are those which we absolutely have to do and those to which we give high value. When I established the value of a clean desk, the initiative came to clean the desk.

You will be surprised what you can do if you assign value to things. If you put a high value on prayer, you will pray. **But you must see the value of doing it or you will not stick to it!** You must value prayer as a source of inspiration, communication, direction, blessing and fellowship. If you put a high value on reading the Bible, you will read it. But you must establish a high value for it. If you put a high value on your family unit, you will make time to spend quality time with your family members. Whatever you put high value on, you will go to any extent to protect and preserve.

For some time I had admired the beautiful Mont Blanc writing pens. However, I realized that the average cost for one was $100 and up. I had admired the pens, but I never invested in one because I felt I might lose it. Then one day I mentioned it to one of my brothers, Bernard. He then invited me into his office and showed me two Mont Blanc pens that he owned. He stated that he owned one of them for about two years and he had never lost it. In fact, when I casually mentioned the pens to him, he knew exactly where both of them were. This was really something for him to keep up with two pens for a long period of time!

As I later thought about it, it dawned on me, "He did not lose those pens because of the high price he paid for them!" That's it. He was able to keep up with the Mont Blanc pens because they have a much, much higher value than an ordinary Bic pen. So you see, you will amaze yourself with what you can do if you place a high enough value on things. Set a value on whatever you need to accomplish. Give it a high value in your heart and mind, and you will do it at any cost!

The value that you give things will even determine your prioritization. If there is something you really value, you will make time to attend to it first. Take your body, for instance. Let's say you are rushing out of the house to get to an important business meeting. As you reach to close the door, you slam your pinkie finger. Now you are in excruciating pain. The bones in your little finger begin to swell. You know your finger is broken. So what do you do? Do you just hold it and rush on to your important meeting? If you are in intense pain due to a broken finger, you will go to the hospital to have something done for your finger. Notice that hurting your little finger can rearrange your priorities. You see, most people would value relieving bodily agony more than getting to an important business meeting.

So if something is suffering in your life, no matter what your current priorities are, you need to change them. If your marriage relationship is suffering at the expense of your career, you need to change your priorities. If your children are suffering at the expense of your career, you need to shift the focus of your attention. If your spiritual relationship with God is suffering, you definitely need to put Him in your itinerary. Whatever the area of hurt, neglect or suffering may be in your life, evaluate its worth to you. If it means enough to you, you will give it your immediate attention.

Sometimes I have been so busy that I worked straight through lunch. I have even worked through dinner. I only did that because the work was important, and I had a deadline to meet. It was important for me to meet my deadline. Eating lunch and dinner did not mean as much to me as meeting my deadline. However, I realized that after a few days of skipping meals, eating became a priority! I had to eat because my energy levels were dropping. My body was weak. Now, what I had postponed was of utmost importance.

Anything of value that you neglect for a long period of time will eventually become your priority. You can put off washing dishes all you want, but when there are no more clean dishes in the cabinet, washing dishes becomes a priority. The same is true with your clothes.

I want you to understand that in order to start a job, you must give it value. Then the value you assign to the job will determine the priority you give it. The priority will then determine when you actually do the job. Setting priorities are necessary to get started with things you would normally procrastinate on.

Starting, however, is only the first hurdle you will need to overcome. After you have started, you have to keep going to get to the finish line. If you will ever run a good race, you do not work on speed. **You need to work on building endurance.** Once you have started something, endurance or perseverance is what takes you to the finish! Of course, to keep your endurance strong, you must keep in mind the value of what you are doing. The value of the thing is a form of reward for you. This is why Paul said, *"I press toward the mark for the prize of the high calling of God in Christ Jesus" (Philippians 3:14).* Paul placed a very high value on the calling in his life. It was such a high value that he gave his life for it.

Once Paul found the truth, he was determined to stick to it. I believe he realized that Jesus was serious when he said, "He that endureth to the end shall be saved" (Matt. 10:22b). As I said, the two most challenging aspects of any job are getting started and getting finished. We have trouble finishing because we lack endurance. Endurance is not automatic. It is something we work to develop. The more you train yourself to endure, the more you are able to endure.

Endurance is a wonderful character trait. It is an imperative asset for any accomplishment. In fact, endurance is perhaps one of the first character traits that we see in God. Remember that in the beginning God created the heavens and earth. For six consecutive epochs, God was busy creating. He had such endurance that He did not rest from His labor till the work was complete.

When I was in school, I was the same way. I could not rest until I completed my school assignments. So when I came home from school, I would immediately begin doing my homework. Despite how long it took, I always finished my homework before I went to bed. Not one time did I ever leave half of my homework undone!

I was driven to endure until I finished my work. Why was this? It was because I put a high value on my education, and I did not want to cheat myself.

You do not have to cheat yourself either. You can learn to endure and you will reap the benefits of the seeds you have sown. How would you feel if you were a farmer who planted acres of land, but never waited for the harvest to come? That would be very sad, but it happens. We invest in some things, and we do not have the endurance to see them through. But we have to take our time and weather the storm. If you want a good crop, you will have to endure rain, cold, heat, pests, dryness and a myriad of other conditions. The bottom line, however, is that you will have a good crop. I know several people who made investments in high interest yielding plans, but they were penalized for early withdrawal. You see, whenever you cannot endure, you will suffer penalties. Paul admonishes that we *"not be weary in well doing: for in due season we shall reap, if we faint not" (Gal. 6:9)*.

I like Paul because he was a positive man. He was a bold man. He was an unrelenting, determined man. He knew how to start a job. But more impressively, he knew how to finish a job. He even trusted that his labor was not in vain, but that it would endure. After establishing the Church at Philippi, Paul wrote the Church saying he was confident of this very thing *"that he which hath begun a good work in you will perform it until the day of Jesus Christ" (Phil. 1:6)*. From this we ought to learn that we should follow through with every good and righteous work we begin. Do not start and stop. Learn to finish and rejoice over the benefits.

The greatest obstacle to completing what we begin is a lack of diligence. Unless you learn to practice consistency with small things, you will never be able to demonstrate diligence with great things. Being diligent is not just something you pick up when you think you need it. It is a habit pattern. You are either a diligent person by habit or you have a sloppy pattern of starting and stopping.

The difference between mediocre and excellence is diligence. With most things, you just have to diligently practice over and over until you reach virtuosity. An 80 year- old virtuoso with the violin was accosted by a young admirer. The youngster had never heard anyone play with such precision. So in great admiration he said to the old man, "I would give my life to be able to play like you." The wrinkled faced man smiled and replied, "I did give my life to play like this!" Then the virtuoso went on to explain how he had practiced for eight hours per day for more than 40 years. Now that is diligence. Diligence is not an overnight sensation. It is painstakingly developed over a long period of time. Diligence prepares with the simmering of a crock pot, not the brevity of a microwave oven. The result is an effervescence with the unmistakable flavor and seasoning that only experience and diligent practice can propagate.

We grow and ameliorate our present abilities by diligently practicing what we know to do. We grow in the Word of God by diligently practicing its truth. By so doing, we mature and have a greater level of discernment.

But evil men and seducers shall wax worse and worse, deceiving, and being deceived. But continue thou in the things which thou hast learned and hast been assured of, knowing of whom thou hast learned them; and that from a child thou hast known the holy scriptures, which are able to make thee wise unto salvation through faith which is in Christ Jesus.
II Timothy 3:13-15

Do you realize that your diligence has something to do with your eternal destination? It takes diligence to be saved. Jesus said, *"...he that endureth to the end shall be saved" (Matt. 10:22b).* The word "endure" in this context is synonymous with "diligence."

Another word that is synonymous with "diligence" is the word "continue." Paul told Timothy, *"Take heed unto thyself, and unto the doctrine; continue in them: for in doing this thou shalt both save thyself, and them that hear thee" (I Tim. 4:16).*

Before you can "continue," or "endure" or be "diligent," you must develop inner discipline. Discipline is a prerequisite for diligence! Jesus said, *"If ye continue in my word, then are ye my disciples indeed" (John 8:31).* A disciple is a disciplined one. So to be a disciple of the Lord is to subject yourself to His discipline of life. But there is no discipline without chastening or chastisement. **Chastening is not punishment, rather it is the teaching of responsibility.** So one connotation of "discipline" is learning to take responsibility for your actions. Disciplined people understand that for every cause, there is a corresponding effect. And for every act, there is a consequence.

So when we want a certain effect or consequence, we must realize that there is something that **we must do.** Everybody believes God has all power and He can do anything because He is sovereign. But I am not talking about what God can do. We know God can do anything. I am talking about what you can do in cooperating with God. You see, we cannot just leave everything in our lives up to God. *"For we are laborers together with God" (I Cor. 3:9a).* Whatever happened to Philippians 4:13? *"I can do all things through Christ which strengtheneth me."* You have a part to do, and God has a part. Otherwise you would have faith without works. We know that *"faith without works is dead"* *(James 2:20).*

Lets take an Olympic athlete, for example. He cannot just pray that he will win the competition without practicing. He has to train as hard as he can. Then he prays and asks for supernatural blessings. He must do his part and trust God to do His part. Remember what Paul said writing to the church at Corinth?

Do you not know that in a race all the runners compete, but [only] one receives the prize? So run [your race] that you may lay hold [of the prize] and make it yours. Now every athlete who goes into training conducts himself temperately and restricts himself in all things. They do it to win a wreath that will soon wither, but we [do it to receive a crown of eternal blessedness] that cannot wither. Therefore I do not run uncertainly — without definite aim. I do not box as one beating the air and striking without an adversary. But [like a boxer] I buffet my body — handle it roughly, discipline it by

hardships — and subdue it, for fear that after proclaiming to others the Gospel and things pertaining to it, I myself should become unfit — not stand the test and be unapproved — and rejected [as a counterfeit].
I Corinthians 9:24-27 AMP

Paul compares his personal discipline with that of a professional athlete. He realized that in order to master anything, you must be temperate in all things. That is, you must use moderation in all things. To be disciplined means to be temperate or moderate with food, sex, television, movies and the like. Discipline suggests regular exercise and going to bed on time. It implies control with spending your money. Most people are not in debt because they do not make enough money. They are in debt because they do not invest it wisely. They impulsively buy what they want. Then they beg, borrow and steal what they really need.

Many people know the value of budgeting, but they lack the discipline to remain on the budget. Discipline is about self -control and moderation. You have to determine what you want to accomplish and constantly remind yourself of it. You have to make sure you do not get out of balance. You can be a workaholic and lack moderation with your career. You can be a sports fanatic and lack discipline to spend quality time with your family. You can even spend too much time doing things in the church and be immoderate. **Having a balanced life with the spiritual, physical, emotional, financial and mental is a beautiful witness for Christ!**

You may say, "I do all right in some areas, but not others." Well, what you need to do is simply work on one area at a time! We become overwhelmed when we try to do too much too fast. So t**ake your time, and work on one area at a time.** If you need some helpful guidelines for building discipline in your life, I will gladly share some with you. Remember, **you must have discipline before you can be diligent.** If you have trouble starting and stopping, I know some simple, practical things that will help you.

The first thing is to **start being disciplined in diligence with a tiny bit.** Then build your way up. It is important to establish a habit pattern of diligence. You see, diligence should be second nature to you. You should not have to think about whether or not you are going to follow through on a project. Being faithfully diligent should be a part of you.

Diligence in small things qualifies you to tackle big things. Remember King David in the Scriptures? Well, as a young man he was the only one brave enough to volunteer to conquer the giant Goliath. King Saul wanted to make sure he was sending a proficient warrior to handle the giant, Goliath. David was just a teen-ager, so what qualified him? David, though young, had a track record. He had been diligent in handling some smaller matters. But King Saul worried about David's competency because he was a shepherd. He even told David, *"Thou art not able to go against this Philistine to fight with him: for thou art but a youth, and he a man of war from his youth" (I Sam. 17:33).* Now how was David to ease Saul's mind? He had to share his track record of diligence. David told Saul in essence, *"I have served as a diligent shepherd for my father's sheep. Once, a lion came and stole one of the sheep. Then a bear stole a sheep. But I recovered both sheep, killing the lion and the bear with my bare hands. And since the Lord delivered me out of the paw of the lion and out of the paw of the bear, I know he will deliver me out of the hand of this giant, Goliath" (I Sam. 17:34-37).*

If David did not have a track record of diligence, King Saul would never have trusted him to conquer Goliath. So the key is to start with the small things first. You do not attempt to conquer a Goliath when you have never conquered a lion or bear. Conquer small things first, and your confidence will grow to conquer great things. Even as a result of David's diligence with sheep, God promoted him to be King over Israel. But do you know what? **Had David not been diligent in handling his father's sheep, God would never have trusted him to shepherd His people.** So you see, God honors faithfulness or diligence.

How does God honor your diligence? He promotes you. He trusts you with more. Remember the parable of the talents? Well, the two men, out of the three, who were diligent with their talents were honored. The master said to both of them, *"Well done, good and faithful servant; thou hast been faithful over a few things, I will make thee ruler over many things: enter thou into the joy of thy lord" (Matt. 25:21,23).* That is a wonderful reward for being diligent over the little you have!

So how do you make all this applicable to your daily life? How do you use this to bring more diligence? Remember to be diligent with the small things. People in authority may not recognize your work with "small things," but they will recognize your diligence. I always recommend starting with small things in your personal life. You see, **the diligence you practice privately will manifest itself publicly!**

If you want more diligence in reading your Bible, do not try reading an hour a day. Start with five or 10 minutes per day. Then gradually increase the time. Likewise, do not start off trying to pray for an hour a day. Again, start with five or 10 minutes for a month to three months. By the third month, the habit of prayer should be established in your life. Once it is established, you can gradually increase the time of prayer. But make sure you make a daily appointment to pray and read the Bible.

I have seen a lot of people start off all excited about doing a new thing in their lives. Then within two weeks, if they can last that long, they become more and more irregular and sporadic. But why? It is generally because they tried to change too much, too fast. Remember, as I said earlier, when you are running a long race, you do not emphasize speed initially. You emphasize endurance. Do you recall the moral in the story of the tortoise and the hare. In that story, we learned that the race is not given to the swift, but to the one who diligently endures to the end.

Taking on too much, too fast will cause you to become discouraged easily. So take your time and make small, comfortable steps that you can handle. Generally, it is not a good idea to make drastic changes. That works for some people, but not most. I knew a woman who attempted a 40-day fast. She had never gone without food for more than a day, yet she thought she could make it 40 days. After the second day, she was so weak that she resumed eating. You see, before attempting 40 days of fasting, try skipping one or two meals a day. Then the next week try a three day fast with water and juice. The following week try three days with water alone. Then the next week, try going four consecutive days without food. Try increasing everything little by little. But before attempting a 40 day fast, I recommend seeking medical supervision.

A couple of years ago, I met a young man who complained constantly about his job and his wages. He said, "I'm a Christian, and I want God to bless me with more money. This job doesn't pay me enough. I make peanuts. They pay me so little that I don't give them half of my best ability." He almost sounded like he was bragging that he did not apply himself on the job because he felt underpaid. I pulled him to the side and said, "Let me get this straight. You want God to bless you with more money and you are not faithful nor grateful for what you have?" He clarified, "Oh, I know this job is better than none at all." After hearing this young man share his viewpoint, I realized he was not a good steward over the money he was making. He threw his money away on frivolity. So I briefly shared with him about being faithful (diligent) in the little things. Being quite frank, I said, "You want God to bless you with mega-bucks,' yet you will not manage your peanuts' first!" After I finished sharing with him, his response was, "I guess I never looked at it like that before, but I understand what you mean." As a result of what I shared with him concerning diligence, he changed his entire attitude toward his job. Within six months, he was promoted to day-shift manager at the fast food restaurant where he worked! You see, there is a reward for being diligent. Sometimes it may take a long time for your diligence to be recognized, but your reward is coming!

The second aspect of being diligent involves **establishing a definite time to be diligent.** If you are going to pray daily, set a particular time for prayer. King David was a man of prayer, but he did not just say, "I'm going to pray sometime everyday." David said, *"Evening, and morning, and at noon, will I pray, and cry aloud: and He shall hear my voice" (Ps. 55:17).* If you want to be a diligent prayer warrior, set a specific uninterruptible time to pray. If you are going to save money, set a specific amount with specific frequency. For instance, "I'm going to put $10 dollars in my savings account from my check every Friday." If you are too general with your commitments, you will never find the time to keep them. You will never find any more time than what you currently have. You simply have to make or reserve time to keep new commitments. You may have to shave 30 minutes from your normal sleeping time to get up and pray, but one thing is sure, **if you do not set a time for what you intend to do, you will never find the time!**

The third aspect of building diligence involves **keeping the reward of your diligence in view.** Remember, there is always a reward for being diligent. The reward of running a race is what motivates you to train so hard and run so fast. A slimmer, healthier body is the reward of adopting sensible eating habits that include a highly nutritious diet (low fat, high fiber with plenty of fruits and vegetables). When you get ready to give up, take another look at the reward you expect. It is good, if possible, to actually get a picture of the reward so that its visual impact will reinforce your purpose. Notice this:

But without faith it is impossible to please Him: for he that cometh to God must believe that He is, and that He is a REWARDER of them that DILIGENTLY seek Him.

Hebrews 11:6

You see, God rewards diligence! He is looking for people upon whom He can depend. When He finds such a people, He rewards their diligence. Diligent people are not quitters. They keep going and going and going. If they do not find what they are looking for in one place, they look in another. They may stop, but only to regroup and strategize. Proverbs 12:24 teaches that the diligent shall bear rule. In other words, they will be your leaders! That is a great reward of being diligent. Here is a good one: *"He becometh poor that dealeth with a slack hand: but the hand of the diligent maketh rich"* (Prov. 10:4). Even Proverbs 22:29 teaches that a man who is diligent in his business will stand before kings. In short, **your diligence will bless your life and cause promotion to come.**

A final suggestion **to help develop diligence is to fast.** Fasting does not change God; it changes you! You can go longer without sex than you can without food. Food is generally the biggest appetite to control. So when you are able to exercise discipline over your appetite for food, you can generally control other animalistic appetites. Food is a focal point in our life. Most of our social functions and big business deals evolve around food. So if we discipline our main uncontrolled area, the pattern is set for other areas to be controlled. I believe this is why fasting and prayer go together so well. If we have the discipline to fast, we also have the discipline to pray! If you diligently moderate your appetite for food, you can diligently pray and read your Bible.

Discipline and diligence, you see, are contagious. When you master them in the main area of your life, the other areas become subordinate. As you fast, you weaken the flesh, but you strengthen the spirit! Give it a try. It works! Soon you will be able to testify that it takes discipline to start, but diligence to finish. With the winning combination of discipline and diligence, you will easily move from start to finish!

CHAPTER 6
Little Foxes Spoil
The Vine

"Heart disease, which is mainly diet related, is a subtle killer. Little by little we destroy our lives. In a very real sense, we are digging our own graves with our teeth!."

Do you realize what destroys health and causes death more than anything else in America? Is it drugs? No, it is not! Is the culprit sexually transmitted diseases? No, it is not. Is it murder and firearms? Wrong again. Is it automobile accidents? No, it is not. Is it by war? I am afraid not. Could it be alcohol? It could be, but it is not. Well certainly it must be from cigarettes. You are wrong again.

The things I just mentioned are conspicuous culprits of bad health and premature death. We know that drugs are extremely detrimental. We fear the horrors of contracting sexually transmitted diseases, especially AIDS. We tremble at the thought of a gun. We pray that God's grace and mercy will spare us as we drive the dangerous streets. We know the odds are stacked against us if we are drafted into war. We have all heard the warnings of indulging in the vices of smoking and drinking. Yet none of these things are the leading cause of death in America!

Well, what is this dreaded terror? It is heart disease! It is commonly and appropriately referred to as "the silent killer." You see, we stand guard against the obvious killers and ignore the subtle ones. Heart disease, which is mainly diet related, is a subtle killer. Little by little we destroy our lives. In a very real sense, we are digging our own graves with our teeth!

The *"Today's English Version of the Bible"* contains *a scripture which says, "Catch the foxes, the little foxes, before they ruin our vineyard in bloom" (Song of Solomon 2:15).* They are the little things, which when left alone, can add up to big danger. We are vigilant over the obvious killers. But we are very unpretentious when it comes to caution with silent, subtle killers.

The little things are the culprits that undermine our infrastructure. Think about it. If we see a spider or a roach in our house, we will kill it to keep our homes pest-free. Yet we will rarely ensure that little things, like termites, are not destroying the house from the inside out. You see, little things do not work on the surface. They work internally. They work subconsciously. They work systemically. They work gradually.

Disease is generally caused by a microscopic bacteria or organism. You cannot even see it with your naked eye! It is hard to believe that something that small can snuff out your life. As a result, we give more attention to pimples that surface on our faces than to lumps that may develop in our bodies. They are the little foxes that spoil the vine!

Therefore, when Satan wants to do something, he does not come as a big devil. He comes as a little, sly fox. Satan is very subtle. The changes he brings come very gradually. He diverts our attention little by little. Then one day, you wake up and wonder, "How in the world did I get in this condition?" People who lose fellowship with God do not do it overnight. They get slack day by day and week by week. They begin skipping their time of prayer. They become irregular in reading the Bible. They start skipping church services. Then before they realize what has happened, they are out of fellowship with God.

You have to be very careful about minding the little things. When the little things get out of hand, the big

things will soon follow! What generally destroys marriages is minutia. I mean, Satan will use every available
little thing to irritate and exasperate marriage partners.
And, of course, the older you are, the less tolerant you
are of little things that aggravate you. Once you reach a
certain age, whatever comes up, comes out. So Satan
does not get us suddenly. He chisels away at us, little by
little.

Remember how Satan deceived Eve? He distracted
her attention and made her look at the forbidden fruit.
Then he posed a provocative question and let her meditate on the temptation. He wanted to get her in the realm
of human reasoning so he could destroy her faith in what
God had commanded. Satan spoke some truth, but he
mixed it with "little" white lies. Those "little" white lies
led to the downfall of all humanity.

We always have to be very wary of little things.
Watch for signs of little things that are moving in the
wrong direction. Nip them in the bud, before they can
bloom. The earlier you deal with potential hazards, the
better. There will never be an opportune time to stop or
correct something that spells trouble. **As soon as you
smell something foul or detect something wrong, stop
it!** As little things come up, deal with them and
move on.

Just take everything a little at the time. That reminds
me of the adage which says, **"Life by the yard is hard;
but life by the inch is a cinch."**

Many parents watch "little foxes" consume their children, while diminishing the significance of the "little
foxes." Seeds of disrespect emerge at young ages, but

many parents dismiss those little foxes as "cute." Sometimes when little foxes emerge, parents think that "this is just a phase; and it will pass." But birthing children out of wedlock is not a phase! Developing a sexually transmitted disease is not a phase! Being strung out on drugs is not a phase! Drunk driving is not a phase! Disrespect and blatant rebellion are not phases! These are very damning habits that will shape lifestyles.

In a certain sense of the word, ignoring these detrimental "little foxes" in children is a form of child negligence. To ignore possible dangers in our lives or in the lives of our loved ones is to welcome the danger. You see, love is about protecting. Love is about disciplining. So when we discipline, we are trying to protect our children from things that can lead them in the wrong direction and destroy them.

When most things collapse suddenly, we have the propensity to think that destruction is immediate. But it is not! Somewhere down the line, there was a small leak or an erosion or deterioration in the foundation. This is where the devil seeks to do his work. **He wants to destroy the foundation.** The Psalmist asks the question, *"If the foundations be destroyed, what can the righteous do?" (Ps. 11:3).* The dismal truth to the question is that we can do nothing without a properly fortified foundation. You see, the most serious dangers in life are practically hidden. Cosmetic damage is generally very superficial and rarely crucial.

Have you ever noticed how long some people can make it with bad health habits before they break down? Some people can smoke, drink, do a few drugs, eat fried and high cholesterol foods for years before they finally fall out with a heart attack. Remember, the devil's plot is to tear you down so slowly that you will not realize anything is happening until it is too late. There are initial warning signs, but we dismiss those as "little, harmless foxes."

Just because something is little does not suggest it is harmless. A termite is little, but it can cause big damage. That is exactly why the wisest man who ever lived, Solomon, said, "Catch the foxes, the little foxes, before they ruin our vineyard in bloom." Your vineyard is your life support system. It is the place you reap God's blessing in your life. Jesus said, *"I am the true vine" (John 15:1a).* **So if you are not careful, little foxes will destroy your perception and understanding of Jesus!** In Scripture, foxes have been a symbol of destruction and false prophets or doctrine. In Luke 13:32, Jesus refers to Herod as a fox, and that is not a good sign. When you address someone as *"You little sly fox,"* that is synonymous with saying, "You little sly devil."

Although "little foxes" may present themselves to be harmless, they are just the opposite. When things are stolen little by little, you barely notice anything missing. Of course, anyone would notice if an entire room of furniture had been burglarized. But if a small ceramic item were stolen or a certain book or CD, you would not notice it immediately. In fact, you probably would not notice a small item being gone until it is time to use it again.

Most people do not budget themselves well because they spend a lot of money on several inexpensive items.

But what they do not realize is that those inexpensive items add up. Two dollars here and five there will add up to all your extra money very quickly. Buying little things which are not on your grocery list can skyrocket your checkout total. So never underestimate how quickly little things add up.

A few years ago, I noticed a hole in a water line in my basement. The hole was about the size of a sewing needle. Since it was so small, I ignored it. Well, not only did that hole cause the carpet to get soaked, it caused my water bill to be about $230 more than normal. That incident taught me the value of attending to things while they are small. Now, I really understand the statement, "An ounce of prevention is worth a pound of cure."

If you are not vigilant over little things, big problems can emerge. You may struggle desperately to lose weight over several months. Yet, when you reach your desired weight, you must remain conscious of keeping off extra pounds. Weight is shed very gradually, but it slips on very quickly. You do not notice a significant change in weight just because you eat a sinfully delicious dessert. So you eat another and another and another until you notice an increase. Then one day you notice that your clothes do not fit comfortably. After you have put on a few additional pounds, you cannot retrospectively decipher which meal caused the gain. The gain from each meal was so small that you did not register it as a hazard to weight control. So you see, ignoring a small problem can result in a greater problem. Anything that increases or decreases little by little is difficult to track without making a determined, cognizant effort.

I now realize that little things can teach a big lesson. In fact, the genuine truth about things is not found in the great aspects of life, but in the little things. If I really want to know something about the character of a man, I do not look at how well he does his job. I do not consider the worth of his reputation in the community. I do not even judge it by his involvement in the church. Rather, I check to see how he relates to his wife and children. If his immediate family loves and respects him, he is generally a man of genuineness and quality. You can tell much more about a man by the way he treats his wife and children than by the way he treats his job!

If a woman wants to know how a man will treat her as a wife, she should take note of how he treats his mother. If a man disrespects his mother, he will disrespect his wife. If a man expects his mother to do everything for him (cook, clean, wash clothes, etc.), he will expect the same from his wife. By the same token, if a man wants to know something about the way a woman will relate to him as a husband, he should observe how she relates to her father. If she manipulates her father for what she wants, she will manipulate her husband. If she adores and serves her father, she will do the same toward her husband. Of course, these are general truths, which means there are many exceptions. But I have found that there is a great parallel between the attitudes of children toward their parents and the attitudes of those same children toward their spouses.

Little things make a big difference! For us to be extraordinary, all we need is a little "extra." It does not always take a great deal more. **If we will simply sacri-**

fice to do a little extra with everything we do, we will be distinguished as extraordinary! You do not have to be common. Put a little extra in what you do and become extraordinary! Yes, all it takes is a little extra in what you ordinarily do to make you exceptional. It is not nearly as hard as you think. I have talked with some people who have accomplished great things. Yet, when I asked them how they do extraordinary things, they really cannot adequately explain it. I have found this to be so because they do not see themselves as extraordinary. To them, it is ordinary for them to do what they do. Some people just naturally have better discipline and motivation than others. Some people naturally do more than what is expected of them. They do not wait until they are told to do things that obviously need to be done. Having this type of attitude sets a person apart. It causes a person who is ordinarily self-motivated to be considered extraordinary.

Extraordinary people are such a rare breed because most people will not do the little extra things without compensation or recognition. Most people who are asked to do something that is beyond the call of duty want to know how much overtime they will be paid. That is an ordinary attitude and response. But an extraordinary person will work beyond what he is paid to do without the boss knowing about it. Then the little extra effort he has put forth will manifest in his work and attitude. Eventually, those in leadership will recognize the extra effort and promote that person.

If you have two people who are equally qualified for a job, how do you choose the right candidate for the one

opening you have? If the educational background and
the experience of the two individuals are comparable,
how do you make a decision? Well, when the major
things in their lives are parallel, you have to look at
details. Which one seems to have the better attitude?
Who seems to be more likely to put forth the "little
extra"? Who seems to be more energetic? Which seems
to be better organized? Take a hard look at the little
things in the personality, attitude and appearance and
make the decision. The little things will tell you which
one will be better in the long run.

I have a set of identical twin girls. Whenever we are
out with all our children, people ask us, "How do you
tell them apart?" Well, we are able to distinguish them
by little things that make a big difference. We know that
one twin is physically bigger than the other. One twin
sucks her thumb; the other does not. One twin's personality is a little more outgoing than the other. One
twin has longer hair than the other. My wife and I readily notice these differences. Yet, strangers find it impossible to distinguish the two. You see, my wife and I are
more sensitive to the differences in our twins that make
them unique. We see them as distinctly different without making comparisons. They are the little things that
show their differences. One is not better than the other,
they are just different.

Some people can see some of the distinguishing fac-
tors in my twins. One lady said, "They look just alike,
but one is bigger than the other!" I often say, "Whatever
follows the **'but'** is the most important part of what is
stated." "But" is a little word that makes a lot of differ-

ence in what is said. You may ask someone to go with you to a program. The person will reply, "I would really love to go with you to your program, **but** I promised my mother I would help her clean out her garage tomorrow." The bottom line about what you want to know is what follows the **"but."** Always learn to put your emphasis on what follows the **"but."** The Scripture says *"...weeping may endure for a night, **BUT** joy cometh in the morning" (Ps. 30:5b).* That means we are not to concentrate on the weeping part which only endures for a night. Rather, we are to focus on the joy which is coming in the morning! Remember to focus on what follows the "but." Another scripture says, *"Many are the afflictions of the righteous: **BUT** the Lord delivereth him out of them all" (Ps. 34:19).* Again, that means we are not to concentrate on the afflictions that come in the life of the righteous. Rather we are to focus on the fact that the Lord delivers us out of every affliction! This is what follows the **"but."** **"But"** is a little word, yet it represents a major turning point for us.

Little things in life are like seeds. They have all the characteristics of the full grown tree. So all we have to do is water the little things — be faithful with them — and they will grow. If a big thing is made of quality little things, you will have a quality big thing. You see, the whole thing is the sum of its parts. This is why it is so important to be faithful and diligent in the little things. If we cultivate the little things properly, they will mature into wonderful plants and trees that will bear innumerable fruit!

The little seed determines what the big tree will look

like. So do not underestimate the importance of the little things. If I am going to sit outside and do some work, I like to know the direction of the wind so I can position myself appropriately. I do not look at big office buildings or houses to determine which way the wind is blowing, I look at the direction of a leaf as it vacillates in the wind. The small things that move with the wind tell the direction, not the big things. So learn to pay attention to the small details because the little foxes can ruin your vineyard in bloom if you are not careful.

CHAPTER 7

Casting Out
FAT Demons

"I could tell by her expression and gestures that she prayed with the authority of an army sergeant."

A few years ago, I went out to lunch with a young lady who practiced a peculiar method of weight control. We sat down in a moderately-priced restaurant and ordered our meals. After approximately 15 minutes, the casually attired server brought our entrees to the table. I quietly bowed my head and gave thanks for my food. As I looked up, I noticed the young lady was jerking back and forth, waving her hands over her food as though she were casting an incantation. With eyes tightly closed, she deliberately moved her lips as she muttered her grace. Although I could not discern every word, I could tell by her expression and gestures that she prayed with the authority of an army sergeant. With her mouth open, tongue moving and lips balled tightly against her teeth, I heard her say "I rebuke you...!"

Finally after about three and a half minutes, my lunch companion brought her grace to an end. She simply looked up at me and said, "Oh, this looks good," and began eating. Well, I just could not resist asking her what on earth she was doing in her prayer. She replied, "You see, I'm having a little challenge with my weight. And I realize that food doesn't make me fat, but there are fat demons in the food that try to make me fat. So I was just casting out the fat demons. That way I can eat whatever I want without gaining excess weight."

I thought to myself, "This is about the most bizarre thing I have ever heard." But without trying to be judgmental, I very light-heartedly said, "I'm afraid this kind (of demon) only comes out by prayer **and fasting.**" Then we discussed the biblical account of the time when Jesus' disciples had trouble casting a demon out of a boy. So when Jesus cast the demon out, his disciples asked why they could not. Of course, Jesus' response was, *"this kind goeth not out but by prayer and fasting" (Matt. 17:21).*

After a rather lengthy discussion, I was able to help the young woman to understand that you cannot control weight through casting out "fat demons." You see, I found out that the woman had been casting out fat demons for about two years. But the grim reality was that she was still over her desired weight level. I looked straight in the woman's eyes and said, "A demon is not interested in possessing food. He is only interested in possessing a person." But, one thing is sure: you cannot cast out a "fat demon." You can bind fat in a girdle. You can cover it with loose fitting clothes. You can wear patterns that camouflage it. You can laugh about it, joke about it, and learn to walk around holding it in. Or you can ignore it, but you cannot hide it!

When people have eating disorders or food addictions, they do not have a problem with demons in their food, they have a problem with uncontrolled internal desire. In other words, **when our internal controls are functioning properly, we have no problem controlling our external influences.** You may have a problem with your genetic build. You may have a problem with your metabolic speed. You may even have a problem with certain glands which help regulate weight. But you do not have a problem with a "fat demon."

Is it really fair to assign the devil responsibility for everything that we do not discipline ourselves to control? I am the first to concede that there are a few extreme cases where complete demonic possession precludes a person from controlling his actions. Yet this type of person is perhaps the only one who could justifiably say, "The devil made me do it!" (like comedian Flip Wilson used to say in the '70s). So then the rest of the population, which is not demon possessed, must take responsibility for its own actions. Despite the tragedies and horrors of our background and experiences, we can control ourselves! No matter how challenging our present circumstances are, we can control how we respond to them! **We may not be able to control the actions of others, but we can at least control our reactions to others.**

I have never had a problem accepting overweight people. So whatever I say about getting a grip on your appetite is not intended to condemn, criticize nor humiliate. It is merely to help, exhort and instruct. Not only am I trying to help the overweight, but also the average weight and underweight who also have problems with appetite control. You see, I realize that many gluttons are not fat! And being fat does not necessarily mean unhealthy, just as being thin does not necessarily imply health. Of course, being grossly overweight is unhealthy. I do not believe that you should allow standard charts to define what is right for you. You are a unique individual. Just because you may be 5'7" tall, does not mean you should weigh the same as another person of the same height. You have a different genetic make-up and a different bone structure. So there may be quite a variation from person to person. However, if you do have a problem controlling your appetite (whether you eat too much or too little), you can do something about it! In some cases you may need medical assistance, but generally you can do something about your situation!

One of the first things that overweight people tend to do about their situation is to use euphemisms to make their status sound more palatable. So the term "fat" becomes "obese." "Fat" becomes "overweight." "Fat" becomes "love handles." "Fat" becomes "full-figured." Among other things "fat" becomes "pleasantly plump, healthy, and big-boned." You can change the name all you want, but the result will not change. So please do not be offended when I use the term "fat."

When you think about it, what was the very first thing that got Adam and Eve in trouble (Genesis 3:1-6)? It was food. What did they eat? Forbidden fruit. It was forbidden because it would be detrimental to their life. What was the bartering tool that Jacob used to deceive Esau out of his birthright (Genesis 25:29-34)? It was food, a bowl of lentil beans. Food has contributed to the downfall of many. The night Babylon fell, Belshazzar threw a big feast which turned into a drunken brawl (Daniel 5:1-31). Even Eli's sons were killed because they loved fat and would steal it from the sacrifices of the Lord (I Samuel 2:27-34). I honestly think they were gluttons. They were out of control. As a result, they had to die. The Lord told Eli that he would judge his house *"because his sons made themselves vile, and he restrained them not (I Samuel 3:13)."*

I believe gluttony in any form, whether with eating or drinking, is sinful. Remember Adam and Eve were charged with sin because they allowed their appetites to supersede obedience to the Lord. With gluttony, you lose control of yourself. As I often say, **when you lose control, the devil finds it.** So if you are out of control in some area of your life, you should not judge others who are out of control in certain areas of their lives. **By this, I mean anyone who cannot control how much he eats is not in a position to criticize or condemn anyone who cannot control how much he drinks.** You may argue and say, "At least I'm not hurting anybody when I overeat." But the truth is that gluttony does hurt someone, it hurts you! You get sick. Then your family suffers with you. Your job suffers. Your income suffers. The insurance company suffers. And ultimately, the other policy holders suffer with higher premiums.

America is perhaps the most over-fed nation in the world. We are digging our own graves with our teeth. I believe diet-related illnesses kill more people than all the illegal drugs combined. As a result of ministering to thousands over the years, I have discovered that more people die and are sick from excess weight and a lack of discipline in their appetite than from any other source. This is why one of the first things the doctor will do after a thorough physical exam is to restrict your diet. Based on your diagnosis, the doctor will tell you, "No fried foods. No salt. No sodas. No alcohol. No sugar. No eggs. No red meats. No fats, greases or oils." You see, when we abuse things, we lose things. We no longer eat just to nourish our bodies. We eat to celebrate, entertain and placate our sweet tooth. We eat too much of the

wrong types of food. Why do we keep doing this to ourselves? We have simply lost control of the situation.
Things have gotten out of hand (our hands). But thank
God we can put it back in His hands. You know, when
man was created from the dirt of the earth, he was given
dominion and authority over all the earth. When you
think about it, all our food comes from the earth. Our
vegetation, fruits, nuts and grains come from the earth.
Even the animals we eat are herbivores (vegetarians).
We are to rule and have dominion over the earth and
everything in it! But we have allowed the earth and its
products to take dominion over us. Now many are at the
mercy of tobacco (cigarettes), marijuana, cocaine, hero-
ine, and alcohol, which all come from the earth. Even
simple things like cocoa beans and coffee beans dominate us. Some people cannot control the urge to have
something chocolate in their mouth. Others cannot get
going for the day without their morning cup of coffee.
We allow the earthly elements, that we are supposed to
have dominion over, to dictate to us when to eat and
drink and how much.

When you do not understand who you are or what
authority you possess, the earth and life's situations will
always rule you. **Either you change the circumstances
or the circumstances will change you!** Sometimes you
may not know why you are eating. All you know is that
you have a taste for something. At times you really may
be hungry for love or attention, but you try to fill that
craving with food. So while you are trying to get a grip
on your appetite, you should also try to improve your
personal relationships.

If you really want help in controlling tendencies toward gluttony, I have a few suggestions. First, **keep yourself occupied with wholesome activities.** Budget time to read the Bible, pray and study material that will help you to be a better person. The Bible teaches that *"an idle soul shall suffer hunger (Prov. 19:15)."* The soul is comprised of the mind, the will and the emotions. So it is good to keep your mind busy, your will exercised and your emotions filled with love and joy. You can notice that idle people are hungry people. When you are not busy, you tend to think more about food. But sometimes when you really have a lot of work that you want to accomplish, you can work right through lunch without realizing it. So when you learn to keep yourself occupied, you do not have as much of a problem with food cravings. Anyway, a craving is a sign that you have a deficiency of a vital nutrient. When my wife was pregnant with our first child, she craved a bizarre mixture of orange juice mixed with ice cream. My wife did not realize that this was a legitimate craving until I convinced her to try the mixture after she had the baby. She tried it and did not like it! But obviously there was some nutritional value in the orange juice and ice cream that the baby needed.

The second key to getting a grip on your appetite is to **eat to satisfy hunger, not to stuff yourself.** *"The righteous eateth to the satisfying of his soul: but the belly of the wicked shall want (Prov. 13:25)."* You either eat till you are satisfied and quit or you go beyond that point and satiate yourself. We normally go beyond satisfaction because everything tastes so good. Sometimes we go beyond satisfaction because we do not want to waste money.   Other times, perhaps, it is because we were trained as children to eat everything on our plates. **Regardless of how you were raised, if you discover that something you are doing is detrimental, stop it and change!**

The third key is to **make a determination, as an act of your will, to set limits for your appetite.** The wisdom of the proverbs encourages us to *"...put a knife to thy throat, if thou be a man given to appetite (Prov. 23:2)."* I like to paraphrase that verse this way: "If thy appetite offend thee, slit thy throat." Certainly no one should take that literally! I believe that verse is telling you to put as much pressure on yourself to control your appetite as the point of a knife pressing on your throat would. Discipline is the salient factor. Over-indulgence is the problem. *"It is not good to eat much honey [sweets] (Prov. 25:27)."* But it is a good idea to *"Be not among winebibbers; among riotous eaters of flesh [meat] (Prov. 23:20)."* In other words, these two verses warn against too many **sweets** and too much **meat!**

A fourth practical suggestion in controlling your appetite is **never eat to feed depression.** When you are depressed, you lose your emotional stability.   Your thinking is not fully rational. You develop a rather insouciant, apathetic attitude. You let all your guards down. If you are depressed, call a friend who can make you feel better. Read something inspirational. Look at a comedy show. Go to church. Try anything wholesome, but do not resort to eating to make you feel better. Try exercising or helping someone who is less fortunate.

Sometimes it will help to just make yourself bless the Lord and praise His name! I tell you, rejoicing releases joy! Joy is better than food any day, especially when you are not suffering from genuine hunger. *"All the days of the afflicted are evil: but he that is of a merry heart hath a continual feast (Prov. 15:15)."* You can feast off your joy! Eat when you are happy. Your food will be a feast to you, even if it is crackers and water! Furthermore, if you are happy, it will digest much easier. That is why *"Better is the dinner of herbs where love is, than a stalled ox and hatred therewith (Prov. 15:17)."*

A few years ago, I went to the house of a fellow minister to pray for his healing. Upon entrance of his house, I discerned that he needed to make adjustments in three areas of his life. First I told him, "You have bitterness in your heart toward your wife that you need to resolve and release." He nodded his head and turned his face to the wall, putting his hand over his mouth and nose. He wept silently. Secondly, I said, "You have not been accountable with finances, neither in the church nor in your home. You must cease stealing through negligence and poor accounting practices." Thirdly I said, "Unless you drastically change your diet, you will be dead before this year is out." Without any exaggeration, he was already well over 500 pounds! I do not know the measure of his success in the first two areas. But his wife told me, "He will not eat anything wholesome. He wants everything fried and greasy." Within six months this man, in his early 40s, was dead due to problems associated with his obesity. I realize I cannot help everybody. I help whom I can. You may not be able to help others , but you can do something about yourself!

I believe the perfect place to start anything is with self. Self is the one area over which we have responsibility and control. There is no need in my discussing anything I cannot change. My philosophy is simple: **Do what you can with what you have.** Use what you have. You have a will, a mind, a body, a spirit, creativity, imagination, determination, intuition, enthusiasm, talents galore, integrity and the list goes on. But most of us do not even scratch the surface of our hidden potentials, our capped capabilities, our untapped strengths nor our unused resources. Yet within every obese person, there is a slimmer person aching to get out. Within every sloppy person is a neat person who wants to use his innate skills of organization. Within every timid man is a lion who roars to express himself. We, like a sculptor, simply have to be willing to remove valuable chunks of our marble until an image of who we really are surfaces. Then others will discover the fascinating work of art that was within us all along.

Change is what we need when we are out of control in a certain area of our life. That is all the sculptor does with his hunk of stone or marble. He changes it until it looks like the image that he has in his mind. We must do the same thing. **We keep changing until we externalize what we have internalized.** But keep in mind that change is progressive. We do not abruptly change from "A" to "B." Going from "A" to "B" may require 10 different changes before you get to "B."

Sometimes we need a stimulus in order to make us change. A group of kids making fun of a fat lady may

provide the needed initiative to changing her mind about
her eating and exercise habits. For another fat lady it
may take growing out of many of her clothes and the
expense of new clothes which spark the change. Yet in
order for another fat lady to change, her doctor may have
to tell her that her life is in jeopardy. Even a failed
romantic relationship can be used as a catalyst for
change. So when adversity or ridicule happens to you,
do not get mad, get smart — and change! I do not recommend changing to suit others. That can make you
very unstable. **Change to suit yourself and your God.**
Whatever it takes to motivate change in you, use it! This
book can do it! The right message on a cassette can do
it. Attending a certain kind of a seminar can do it. A
dynamic church service can do it. **Whatever impetus
you need, get it and use it!**

Do you feel as if you are dealing with a "fat demon"
in some area of your life? Remember that fat is not a
demon. I believe it is a tangible, physical substance or
condition that you can generally do something about if
you really want to. Fighting fat may be a real war for
you, but you can be victorious if you fight with the right
strategy. As you begin your fight, it is important to realize that spiritual warfare is done in the spirit just as physical warfare is done in the flesh. However, out of a disciplined spirit comes a disciplined mind. And out of a
disciplined mind comes a disciplined body. Therefore,
if you believe the right things (concerning your body) in
your spirit, you will think the right way (concerning
your body) in your mind. Of course, how you think will
determine how you will act with your body. So I intend

to impact your spirit with things that will change your thinking, and hence, your actions. But please understand that change will not just happen. We set our wills for change. I agree wholeheartedly with Mike Murdock who says, "If you want something you have never had, you must do something you have never done."

Let today be an identifying mark for a change in your life. Getting started is the first battle you must fight. Sticking to the battle through perseverance is the pivotal point of the entire war. Then getting finished is the culminating battle that will bring you victory! Start slowly. Build momentum and establish good habit patterns. Soon you will be in store for a glorious and rewarding finish. It is always hard in the beginning, but that phase will pass. **"The only place that you start out on top is when you are digging a hole,"** was the advice of a friend of mine. That makes a lot of sense, doesn't it?

Step by step is the way we walk to the reward of a disciplined, more organized life. We gradually transform our thinking, which gradually transforms our life. Yes, little by little a "fat mentality" is transformed into a "slim mentality." You see, a "fat mentality" feels compelled to eat everything on the plate. Whereas a "slim mentality" will eat until it is satisfied and request a carry-out container. **The "slim mentality" knows when to quit!** When a very successful gambler was asked the secret of his success, he replied, "When I'm hot, I'm hot. And when I'm not, I quit!" **It is vital for us to know that moderation and balance are imperative for success in any area. Plainly, we must learn when to quit!**

When you think about a delectable piece of cake, you do not think in terms of how tasty the eggs are or the flour or the milk or the sugar is. You think about the cake as a blend of all the ingredients which gives pleasure to your taste buds. But it is the proper balance of the ingredients that makes the cake good. Too much salt, baking soda, nutmeg, or vanilla extract will throw off the balance of the whole cake. Then people will say, "That cake was too rich and spicy."

Not only must there be a perfect blend of ingredients, **the environment must be right for your cake to turn out right.** With all the right ingredients, you can bake your cake too fast or for too long and dry it out. So when you try a new regimen, take your time, not only to get the right ingredients, but to make sure the environment is right. You may have a fabulous health plan to get a grip on your weight, but your environment may not be proper. You may have the best diet plan and exercise plan, but you cannot stay with it because your environment is wrong. Sometimes the privacy of your home is the wrong environment for you to try to exercise. You may need to get out to a gym where other people are exercising in order for you to be motivated by your environment. Otherwise, you will have hundreds of dollars worth of exercise equipment just sitting in your home getting rusty. The key to your program of change "baking " correctly may be establishing a friendship with someone who has done or is trying to do a similar thing. You see, success attracts success. Money draws money. So if you plan to go anywhere, get with someone who is going somewhere.

Cast out your "fat mentality" and slip into something a little more comfortable. Make up your mind to get a grip on yourself! Make a daily effort to consciously crucify the "fat man" within! It will get hard sometimes, but we must be harder. It is hard because most things with high percentages of saturated fat are good to us. But what we must keep in focus is: **Not everything that is good to us, is good for us!** So we must learn to be very discriminating about what and how much we ingest and imbibe.

To make changes for better personal discipline, you will need to set objectives for yourself. Set your objectives first. Don't just say "My, my, I sure have gained a lot of weight. I need to go on a diet." You see, talk alone will never change your situation. If the circumstances of your life are going to change, you will be the one to put that change in motion by your own determination! **It is totally within your jurisdiction to set the objectives for your life.**

Objectives give a sense of direction to your life. Your objectives tell you where you want to go or what you want to achieve. An objective is very broad, so you will need to set goals to achieve your objectives. Goals are more specific. They are your practical plans of actions to realize your objectives. I believe the major difference between an objective and a goal is that a goal is measurable. You may set an objective by stating, "I'm going to lose 10 pounds." Next, you set your goals for how you will achieve these goals by stating something like, "I will jog five miles every morning from 6-7 a.m. I will drink a gallon of water daily and eat three meals of 350 calories or less. Hence, I will lose two pounds per week for five consecutive weeks." Now those are specific goals for reaching the broad objective of losing 10 pounds. You can very easily measure the progress of those goals by checking to see if you are doing them daily. But without goals, you cannot measure the progress of an objective. **Simply stated, an objective tells you what you want to achieve, whereas a goal tells you how to achieve it.**

Have you set definite objectives for your life? Is it your objective to take authority over the "fat demons" in your life? Have you set specific goals to determine a systematic plan of action? Have you assigned high priority to achieving your objective? These are just a few questions you should ask yourself. Of course, objectives should not be established independently of prayer. Your objectives should also be consistent with biblical principles. *Remember to delight yourself in the Lord so that He will give you the desires of your heart (Psalm 37:4).* But although God has objectives for your life, He leaves considerable room for all your objectives that are harmonious with His.

CHAPTER 8
Work It Out

"After you get beautiful ideas, you need to execute them. Success does not come until you put your ideas in action."

Before you can do anything effectively, you must plan purposefully, prepare prayerfully and pursue persistently. In other words, getting things done is primarily a matter of **preparation and perspiration.** After you get beautiful ideas, you need to execute them. Success does not come until you put your ideas in action.

Most people who conceive good ideas never get specific enough to set a goal to realize their ideas. They usually keep their ideas in the hypothetical or theoretical stage. They say things like, "One day I'm going to..." or "I could really make a lot of money if..." They have good ideas, but they do not have a plan of action to implement those ideas.

To get things from the idea stage to the reality stage requires a long transition period called **WORK!** Yes, the realization of dreams mandates 90 percent perspiration. If you have big plans, you had better be prepared for big work! Whatever you plan on doing has to be worked out! Either you work it out or you die with unfulfilled aspirations.

To complete your work, you will need preparation, inspiration and perspiration. Achievement of any kind requires hard work. You can work smart or you can work hard, but you must work. As Frederick Douglas put it, "You cannot have progress without a struggle." He explained that "those who want progress without a struggle are like those who want a crop without first plowing up the ground. They are like those who want rain without the thunder and lightening."

The bottom line is that if you want something, you

need to pray like a saint and work like a dog! If you are going to bring a greater discipline to your personal life, you are going to have to work at it. You have to work at it one day at a time. Sometimes that requires a lot of sacrifice. **But the good news is that the greater the sacrifice, the greater the blessing!** I mean when you have something that you really want to do or need to do, you have to be willing to work while others are sleeping. You have to sacrifice and be willing to work while others are playing. You have to work while others are on vacation. But one thing is sure: your God directed and inspired work will pay off.

As you work hard, you will get tired, but do not be discouraged. This is normal. When you get tired, you simply need to rest a little and continue working. You cannot afford to rest too long, but you do need to rest! The Lord knows that you will get tired, so he says:

Come unto Me, all who are weary and heavy-laden, and I will give you rest. Take My yoke upon you, and learn from Me, for I am gentle and humble in heart; and you shall find rest for your souls. For My yoke is easy, and My load is light.

Matt. 11:28-30 NAS

I want you to notice that even if you are tired, Jesus does not promise to let you out of work. Rather, He offers to teach you how to work **with** Him instead of **for** Him. Remember *"we are laborers together with God" (I Cor. 3:9a)*. When you try to do things independently of God, life is very hard. But when you are working with God, in accordance to His will, you have grace to endure with much greater ease. On the contrary, *"the way of transgressors is hard" (Prov. 13:15b)*. You see, when you attempt to rebel against God, you make your way very, very hard. Life is always much easier when we submit and learn to cooperate with God's plan.

The lives of many young people have been made hard because they would not listen to godly counsel. They would not listen to their parents or grandparents. They would not listen to their teachers. They would not listen to the Bible. They would not listen to the voice of experience, regardless out of whose mouth it came. As a result, they had to learn simple lessons the hard way. For one woman, it took 10 years and three children for her to realize that her mother was right about her husband. She learned a valuable lesson the hard way. Now she knows that if her head is telling her one thing and her heart is telling her another, she should not trust her feelings over the convictions in her heart.

People learn differently. Some people have to learn the hard way because of their stubbornness. You see, stubbornness causes you to have to work extra hard. You either work properly, with the right attitude, or you prolong your work. In case you have not noticed, it takes a lot of time, energy, money and heartache to learn lessons the hard way.

When Jesus says, "Take my yoke...," He is metaphorically seeing us as an ox. You see, the ox represents work, not food. It was the fatted calf, not the ox, that was dressed for the table. But in Bible days, the ox was the tractor. Even in many under-developed areas of the world today, the ox serves as the tractor. When it comes to working, we should be as strong and dependable as an ox. Our work with Christ or with anyone is not about speed. It is about steadiness and endurance. We are not race horses, but work horses! When it comes to the things of the Lord, the race is not given to the swift. Rather, it is given to him who steadily works and endures until he finishes! Keep in mind **that the method of Jesus Christ is not showmanship, but workmanship!**

Now when Jesus says, "Come unto me all ye that labor and are heavy laden, and I will give you rest," He is not talking about rest in the traditional sense. The rest that Jesus is talking about is not a form of inactivity. Instead it is a form of directed activity! Jesus does not say, "Come unto me all ye that labor and are heavy laden, and I will let you lie down and sleep." No, if you labor and are weary, he says, "Take my yoke upon you and learn of me." In other words, if you are weary, worn and sad from trying to do things your way, then try it Jesus' way! If you have tried, to no avail, to work things out yourself, try yielding to the Lord's way!

Our minds are finite. We do not have all the answers. We cannot afford to lean to our understanding, because our understanding is so limited. So Jesus is telling you, "If you are tired of being disappointed and dissatisfied, try it my way." If you are just working and working, without getting ahead, try it the Lord's way. **Give your way a rest!** If you are tired of the yoke you are in, Jesus is saying, "Put your neck in my yoke and learn from me."

When Jesus says, "Take my yoke...," that is not so much an invitation to learn about Him as it is an opportunity to learn from Him. You see, religion can only teach **about** Jesus. But only an established relationship can put you in a position to learn **from** Jesus. **You will always learn considerably more through relationships than religion could teach in a thousand lifetimes.** You see, it is impossible to be in the same yoke with Jesus, without learning something about being an ox. By being in the same yoke, we learn to respond to Jesus as a person, a partner, not as a philosophy or mere consciousness.

Being yoked to Jesus does not bring an additional burden on us, rather it brings an additional blessing to us. The yoke, which rests on the shoulders of oxen hitched to a plow, was used to distribute the burden of work.   As the oxen pull together, neither is overwhelmed. Being yoked to Jesus does not so much mean that we take on His burdens. It means that He, pulling alongside us, takes on ours. One reason that a lot of people are still yoked in bondage is because they want Jesus to carry all the load. They do not want the Holy Spirit as a paraclete (helper). They want Him to do all the work alone. They want to have all the faith, but none of the works.

No matter whose faith it is, **faith without works is dead!** And "dead faith" does not work for anyone! You cannot just pray and let Jesus carry the workload of the yoke alone. You have to get in the yoke with Jesus and *"work out your own salvation with fear and trembling" (Phil. 2:12b)*.

You may feel, "I'm not fit to be in the same yoke with Jesus." You may think that is an unequal yoking. Well, it is! But guess what? It is not uncommon for a larger ox to be yoked with a much smaller ox. Do you know why? Because this a method of training a young ox. They yoke the experienced with the inexperienced, letting the older teach the younger. Now do you understand why Jesus would say, "Take my yoke upon you, and learn from me"?

Jesus teaches us to work like an ox. He teaches us how to move and when to move. When Jesus begins to move, everything that is hitched to Him moves also. We either have to move with Him or have the plow come right up our backbone. God, as when He led Israel with the cloud, does not work on a democratic principle. He takes no votes nor conducts committee meetings. When He is ready to move, He moves! So if we are in the yoke with Him, we must move when He moves. If we attempt to resist moving, we are liable to be seriously injured. When we are yoked with Jesus, as He turns, so must we. Otherwise, we could have our necks broken.

So how does this turning in the yoke with Jesus relate to our lives? You see, when Jesus turns from a thing, the glory He brought departs. And when the glory is departed, there is no need in hanging around. Not turning when Jesus turns is to remain in a relationship when the love is gone. This is as empty as a balloon without air, a rainbow without color, a fish without water or a flower devoid of fragrance.

When you are in a yoke with Jesus, the yoke offers only one option: to be a partner with Jesus! When you are in the yoke with Jesus, you must learn to eat and drink when the Lord eats and drinks. As the "big ox" bends to eat or drink, this is the only time the yoke will be low enough for you to reach the grass or the water.

Sometimes as I am taking a shower, suddenly, the Lord begins to stop and feed. Right in the middle of my shower, revelation begins to come. I realize the Lord is now feeding, so I position myself to graze by meditating on His revelation. While driving, I have discerned the Lord bending to feed. So without access to pencil or paper, I pause to digest the food of heaven. It seems that the Lord has stopped to feed at some of the most inopportune times, but I have learned not to argue. Sometimes I am in a meeting, or I may even be home asleep, when the Lord stops to feed. It may seem inconvenient to me, but I know it will be good for me. I also know I cannot always get the food when I want it. So I get it when Jesus, the "big ox," stops to feed.

Jesus said, "Take my yoke upon you and **learn from me.**" So if you consider yourself to be a follower of Christ, you need to ask yourself, "What have I learned since I have been in the yoke with Jesus?" If you are yoked with Jesus, you ought to be learning something from Him!

Have you learned that the yoke is too heavy for you alone? Have you learned to keep pace with Him by moving when He moves? Have you learned to turn as He turns, so your neck will not be broken? Have you learned to eat and drink, while He is stopping for food and water? Have you learned that as oxen, we are working ultimately to receive a harvest? Have you learned patience and obedience? Have you learned to keep your mouth closed so you can get some work done and learn from Jesus? Have you learned that there is no better partner, with whom to work, than Jesus?

CHAPTER 9
Strength Of The Weak

"In the same way that there is some bad in the best of us, there is some good in the worst of us. Likewise, the strongest person has some weak points, and the weakest person has some strengths."

In the same way that there is some bad in the best of us, there is some good in the worst of us. Likewise, the strongest person has weak points, and the weakest person has strengths. Practically every time there is a pro, there is a con. There are benefits, and there are drawbacks. There are dividends, yet there are risks of loss. Life is comprised of this kind of unique polarity.

Although there are a few things which require you to be one way or the other, you generally do not have to fit into just one of two molds. You do not have to be classified as traditional or revolutionary, conservative or liberal, aggressive or passive. There is such a thing as "middle ground." In fact the "gray area" is the largest territory in many instances. However, the gray area or middle ground does not necessarily mean that you are guilty of compromising your standards. It simply suggests that you have a blend of certain personality traits. In this case, you can still be all right because moderation is employed.

Marriage is a prime example of a relationship which presupposes a "middle ground." Successful marriages mandate a "give and take" philosophy. There can be differences, but there must be some common denominators. These common denominators form peaceful fields of negotiation and acceptance. But in order to know how far to go to the right or left, you must have maturity and discernment. Life is not all black and white. It is a myriad of living colors, the gray areas being included.

Nevertheless, balance is the key to life. It gives us variety. It keeps the world interesting. Suppose everyone were academically inclined. Who would do our manual labor? Suppose everyone were mechanically inclined. Who would handle our legal work and taxes? Who would write our books? There is a place and a purpose for everyone!

I have noticed that some children have better motor skills development than others. Then I have noticed that some children have better academic and oratorical skills than others. Is one group better than the other? No, they are simply better developed in different areas. Some of it is due to inherent ability. With others, it is solely the result of practice or training.

Use introspection to discover your weaknesses and strengths. Once you discover them, learn to build your life on your strengths. Remember that even the weakest person has strengths. If you concentrate on your weaknesses, you will debilitate your life. If you concentrate on your strengths, you will fortify your life. You must always choose strong things upon which to build. The strong things will support your weaknesses.

I remember meeting a guy named Beaver. He was a slightly different young man. By this I mean he was double-jointed. Most of his schoolmates ridiculed him. They referred to him as though he were deformed. This made Beaver feel awkward and goofy. He was ashamed of the way his bones were made. I noticed that the ridicule damaged Beaver's self-esteem.

While visiting his school, I went over to Beaver and put my arms around his shoulders. I walked down the hall with him and said, "Beaver, you are a special young man. You can do things nobody else can." He said, "I know, but why does everybody always laugh at me?" I replied, "It's because they don't understand you. Really they wish they could do what you can do with your body!" With a look of amazement he asked, "You really think so?" "Sure they do," was my response.

Then I whispered to Beaver, "You know what you should do?" "What?" he inquired. "You should start charging everybody a quarter to see you do unusual things with your body," I suggested. Then I explained, "That way, they will develop an appreciation for your uniqueness." With his eyebrows raised with excitement he said, "I'm going to give it a try."

Beaver was double-jointed in his arms and legs. He could take his left and right hand and interlock his fingers in front of his stomach. With his fingers still interlocked, he could raise both arms above his head and lower them far behind his back. Then he could get in weird positions on the floor with his legs wrapped around parts of his head. Some of the tricks Beaver could do with his legs looked so supernatural that they are ineffable.

A couple of weeks after I had given Beaver the advice about charging people to see his tricks, I saw him in a store. He rushed over to me, smiling from ear to ear, and said, "This is what I got because of what you told me!" I looked down and he was holding three $10 rolls of quarters. He was very proud of himself. Charging people removed the "freak" syndrome he was experiencing and instilled value in his uniqueness. That is a classic example of finding a strength and capitalizing on it.

Do you consider yourself a weak person? Do you

know your strengths? You see, it is very easy to see the strengths and weaknesses of others. But when you look in the mirror of self-evaluation, what do you see? Whether you know it or not, you have strengths. You may be weak to sexual temptations, alcohol, drugs, lust for money and power or anything. **But despite your weaknesses, there is strength!** If you cannot think of any significant strengths you possess, I want to suggest one to you.

I believe the greatest strength of the weak is not to identify yourself with weakness. When it was time for war, the prophet Joel announced *"Beat your plowshares into swords, and your pruninghooks into spears: Let the WEAK say, I AM STRONG" (Joel 3:10).* **The power of the weak is concentrated in the declaration of strength!**

Every weak person has an area of strength. So learn to declare your strengths. Chocolate may be your weakness, but you have some degree of strength in resisting it. Concentrate on that strength. Exercise the weak muscles and soon they become strong muscles. **Your strength lies in your identification with being strong.**

I want you to understand that **our behavior is established by who we perceive ourselves to be.** Who you believe you are determines what you can do and what you cannot do. You can never score well on a test by calling yourself "stupid." Dr. Martin Luther King Jr. said, "It's not what people call you that matters; it's what you answer to." You see, the most important thing does not involve how others view you. The main thing depends on how you see yourself. Furthermore, answering to a certain name gives acceptance to its meaning.

Think about it. How do you view yourself? If there had to be a particular name that sums up your life, what would it be? The name associated with Father Abraham is "Faith." The name associated with Elijah is "Prophecy." The name that comes to mind with Solomon is "Wisdom." Moses reminds us of "Law." Ezekial's life leaves the impression of "Visionary." The main character of John's life is "Love." So if there were one word to describe your life, what would it be?

If you change your name from "Weak" to "Strong," people will remember you for your strength! Remember that your name gives you a distinct identity. In America, we give names because they sound cute. Or we give names to have something to distinguish one person from another. Otherwise, we would holler out a generic "Hey, you!" But in many parts of the world, especially the Middle East, a person's name denotes a little sentence of information. For example the name Moses means "drawn out of water." Not only was that prophetic of him being placed in a basket and set afloat on the water to save his life, but perhaps his name was prophetic of the Red Sea experience. The most significantly remembered event in the life of Moses was the parting of the Red Sea to bring the Hebrews through the midst of the water. The name Jesus means "Jehovah is salvation." Certainly his name was prophetic of his purpose in life.

Remember that your name establishes an identity with who you are. Ever notice what is in the middle of the word "N-A-M-E"? Yes, "AM." Can you see that? The identity of who you are is found in your name!

Once you know who you are, your behavior adjusts.

Whenever God really wanted to change a person's identity and nature, He changed their name! Remember how "Abram" was changed to "Abraham"? Remember how "Jacob" was changed to "Israel"? You see, a change in name represents a change in status or nature. Whenever the military promotes a person, they receive a new name. The name changes from Buck Private to Private First Class to Corporal to Sergeant. With each name change comes a new status and new responsibilities. A new name means new expectations. So **if you do not like your nature or behavior, change what you call yourself and to what name you respond.** See yourself with a new identity. Stop calling yourself "dumb, stupid, lazy, no good, fat-so, big mama, playboy, etc." We produce behaviors consistent with our name.

If you are not confident in who you are, others will try to impose their name on you. People can commit sin against you and leave their name with you. For instance, a perverted man may sexually assault a young girl. Because the perverted man has a dirty name on his mind, he leaves that name with his young victim. As a result, the young girl feels cheap, dirty, unworthy and promiscuous. Since she has received someone else's identity, she acts out that imposed identity. In many instances her life will be driven toward varied types of moral profligacy.

The only way to change a behavior is to change the way one views himself. You change the way you view yourself by changing your name. Your new name will give you a new identity. The Holy Spirit is called the

"Spirit of adoption" (Romans 8:15). When we are born again, He gives us a new name. With the new name comes a new nature. Anytime someone is adopted, there is a legal name change! So when we come into the kingdom of God, we spiritually get a legal name change!

If you were previously known as "weak," your new name is "strong." If you were previously known as "sinner," you are now known as "the righteousness of Christ." I encourage you to renounce any name you do not like. Then affirm who God says you are!

CHAPTER 10
Get Up, Move On

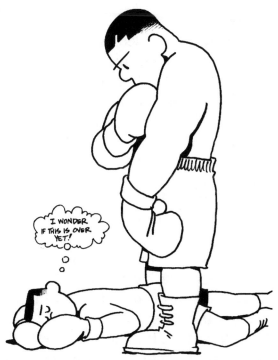

"Many times, after falling, we lie there waiting on someone to help us to our feet. But the truth of the matter is that we can get up, most times, without assistance."

Many times, after falling, we lie there waiting on someone to help us to our feet. But the truth is that most times, we can get up without assistance. Only the aged and the malnourished break bones when they experience a simple fall. So why lie there and wait for sympathy, when you have the freedom and the ability to get up?

Perhaps your pride is more hurt than your body. Perhaps the wind is knocked out of you, and it takes a while to recuperate. You see, when you set your mind to do something, you become disappointed if you do not do it, so the wind is knocked out of you. Maybe you were expecting a "yes," but got a "no." If you are not careful, this can knock the wind out of you too.

If you fail temporarily, do not cease striving! Motivators have repeatedly said, "Winners never quit, and quitters never win!" When you stop to think about it, that really is true. We never really fail, we simply quit trying. So if you want to be successful at becoming a better disciplined person, just keep at it! I am sure it will help you to remember the proverbial saying, "If at first you don't succeed, try, try again!"

Just because you do not succeed the first time you attempt something does not mean it is not meant for you. **When we fall or fail, it simply suggests that we were not prepared well enough for the job.** Failure, no matter how you look at it, results from insufficient preparation. If you fail a test in school, that does not mean you are dumb. It means you did not prepare yourself well enough to pass. A lack of preparation will always cause you to do poorly.

So if you do not succeed at first, prepare more thoroughly for the next attempt. Catch your breath. Pick up yourself, and learn to move on to victory! When you are fighting a war, you are going to lose some of the battles. But a lost battle is no indication of the outcome of the war! Every time you lose a battle, stop to regroup. Wait, so you can clear your head and get a new perspective. Map out new strategies. Evaluate your past mistakes, so you can correct them or at least avoid repeating them. Use your fall for good. There is always something to be learned from it.

When I was growing up, my father hurt his foot on something that was on the floor. He hurt it as he went to the bathroom in the night. From that incident, he made sure we always cleared the floor at night. Ever since then, I have made sure I, at least, have a clear path out of the house and to the bathroom at night. You never know when an emergency might arise. You may have to evacuate the house in the middle of the night. But if the floor is cluttered, you will stumble and hurt yourself, especially your toes. So from my father's experience, I reaped benefits of safety.

You do not have to allow a bad experience to deter you from picking yourself up and persevering. Learn from your experience and keep moving. Do not let guilt and shame paralyze you. You may have messed up, but God does not write you off. You may have sinned, big time, but God is not through with you, yet! Just because you did not stick to your diet, do not make the resolution that "I guess dieting is not for me." If you do not remain consistent with an exercise program or a budget, do not concede "I'm not cut out for this kind of discipline."

If you fall off the horse, get up and ride again! If you are playing baseball and inadvertently fall between bases, get up and keep running! If you stumble and fall, get up and walk again! If you miss the mark, rise up and take a new aim! If you are thrown against the ropes, come back swinging! If something has been lost, get up and restore it! If something good in you has been destroyed, get up and rebuild it!

You see, when you sin, God does not disown you! You are His child. He wants to see you restored, renewed, revived, rehabilitated, regenerated and resurrected! When you think you are through, God is not through with you! After a fall is not the time to sit around and complain. This is not the time to have a "pity party." This is the time to say, "I have to get up from here because my life isn't over yet!" This is the time to say, "I cannot let myself down, my family down or fail my God; I must go on!" You see, God is not merely looking for people who have faith in Him. He is looking for people in whom He can have faith. God wants to be able to depend on us to do His will.

We, like Apostle Paul, should be able to say, *"I have fought a good fight, I have finished my course, I have kept the faith" (II Tim. 4:7).* **It is wonderful to know that as long as you are fighting, you are never defeated!** The minute you cease fighting, a winner is declared. So as long as you are still fighting, you cannot lose! You cannot afford to stay down, whether you were knocked down or you just fell down. You have to get up because you have a course to finish! You cannot give up on your faith, either. You have to keep the faith. **If you keep the**

faith, the faith will keep you!

The Lord does not want you to fail. Neither does He want your faith to fail. Jesus told Simon Peter that Satan desired to have him (Peter) so he could sift him as wheat. But Jesus said, *"...I have prayed for thee, that thy faith fail not: and when thou art converted, strengthen thy brethren" (Luke 22:32).* You see, Jesus did not want Peter's faith to fail. So Jesus prayed for Peter. But guess what? Jesus does not want your faith to fail, either. So He is praying for you and me. How do we know this? *"Who is he that condemneth? It is Christ that died, yea rather, that is risen again, who is even at the right hand of God, who also maketh INTERCESSION FOR US" (Rom. 8:34).* Jesus is praying for you and me because He does not want us to fall.

If we happen to fall, Jesus does not want us to stay down. He wants us to get up and keep moving in Him. We are not to sit around and cry because we fell, but we are to accept His grace and be restored to fellowship with Him. We are encouraged not to sin, but there is a remedy if we do. *"My little children, these things write I unto you, that ye sin not. And if any man sin, we have an advocate with the Father, Jesus Christ the righteous" (I John 2:1).*

We do not rejoice because we fall, but we can rejoice because we can get up and be restored! Remember, **no one drowns because he falls into the water. A man drowns because he stays there!** The good news is that you do not have to stay in the water! There is a life guard on duty waiting to respond to your plea for help. All you have to do is say the word, and your Savior rescues you. He does that because He loves you. You see, love *"rejoiceth not in iniquity, but rejoiceth in the truth; beareth all things, believeth all things, hopeth all things, endureth all things.   Charity never faileth..." (I Cor. 13:6-8a).* **Even when you fail, God's unconditional love never fails toward you!**

I remember privately discussing with a friend the lifestyle of a fellow minister who was involved in open sin. I thought the man should be ashamed of himself. I did not even think he should consider himself a minister. This was not rumor. This was something the minister had confessed to me. The terrible thing about it was that he expressed no regret over his actions. Furthermore, he seemed to have no intentions of stopping his lewd behavior.   I knew nothing of the minister's circumstances. All I knew were his deeds, which he practically bragged about. As a result, I judged this minister. I said to my friend, "He is not worthy even to be called a minister. That man is playing with God. He is going to be struck down." Well, on my way home, I felt convicted of the Holy Spirit concerning what I said about the minister.   Then the Lord conveyed this thought, *"Who are you to judge the servant of another? To his own master he stands or falls; and stand he will, for the Lord is able to make him stand" (Rom. 14:4 NAS).* That message was so clear to me that I pulled over to the side and looked in the back seat of my car. The voice was so real, I thought someone was hiding in the back seat speaking to me.

Well, over a period of four years, God brought a tremendous change in this minister's heart. God caused him to stand. God restored the man because He loved him. Today he is still being used mightily of the Lord. You see, I saw the man in a fallen state, but God saw him in a restored condition! Thank God for what he sees in us. Thank God that He does not readily give up on us!

Jesus had disciples who were not perfect. One of the disciples betrayed Him. Another denied Him. The others forsook Him. Yet, Jesus loved them and was deeply concerned about them. He said, *"I pray for them: I pray not for the world, but for them which thou hast given me; for they are thine. Neither pray I for these alone, but for them also which shall believe on me through their word" (John 17:9,20-21).* You see, not only did Jesus pray for His disciples, He prayed for us. If you believe and have confessed Jesus, it is because He prayed for you. Despite what you have done or failed to do, Jesus is praying for you! He does not want you to fail. If you are down, He does not want you to stay down. He wants you to get up and move forward with Him!

Not only is Jesus praying for you, He moves on the hearts of others that know Him to pray for you, too! From time to time, God will lay a burden on my heart to pray for a particular individual. I know when that happens that there is a degree of danger in that person's life. For instance, one day a fellow, whom I had not heard from in months, came strongly on my mind around 5:45 in the evening. I had a strong urge to intercede on his behalf. Actually, it was more like travailing in the Spirit to give birth to something. I was driving home at the time. As I drove, I interceded for this fellow. I prayed, "Lord, although so-and-so is not living in your will right now, have mercy on him. Protect his life from tragedy and accident..." The travail in prayer became so intense that I pulled over to the side of the road and stretched across the seat to finish praying. After about five minutes of praying, I felt the burden lift from me. So I drove home.

Guess who called me the next day? Yes, this same fellow I interceded for the day before. In a high-pitched, excited voice he said, "Guess what happened to me yesterday! I was rushing home from work and a tractor trailer totaled my car. My whole roof was just ripped off the car. I didn't have on a seat belt and something pushed me down flat on the seat. I didn't get hurt at all!" The only thing I wanted to know was, "What time did the accident occur?" He said, "It was about 6:00 p.m." Then, the only thing I said to him after that was, "You had better thank God for having mercy on you!" He immediately admitted, "Yea, I guess the man upstairs was looking out for me!"

Of course, the "man upstairs" was looking out for him. The Lord was looking out for him because He loves him. God our father, just like any other parent, wants to see His children do well. If we fall, the Lord and the heavenly host stand up in the grandstand and holler, "Get up! You can make it! Run! Run!" You see, all of heaven wants the best for you. Although you may feel as though you are running this race alone, you have much more support than you can ever realize. I have heard people who have fallen say, "I have got to do this for my mother." Their mother may have already gone home to be with the Lord. But there is an encouragement that comes from the Lord and His saints. Just a seed that an ancestor deposits in your life can motivate you to get up and move on!

While there are good influences in life to encourage you, there is also the devil to make you feel terrible about falling. He tries to make you feel like a failure so you will never try to succeed again. He destroys your confidence and self-esteem. He makes you feel unworthy. He brings guilt, shame and condemnation. But remember, *"God sent not His Son into the world to condemn the world; but that the world through Him might be saved" (John 3:17).* **God is not interested in condemning you! He is interested in seeing you saved and delivered.**

If your life seems dismal and black, remember, the picture is not yet complete. The black part that you see is just for a background so the glorious parts will reflect brighter! *"For from of old, men have not heard, nor perceived by the ear, nor has the eye seen a God besides You, Who works and shows Himself active on behalf of him who [earnestly] waits for Him" (Isa. 64:4 AMP).* In other words, you cannot tell from your current status what God is going to do in your life. John put it this way, *"Beloved, now are we the sons of God, and it doth not yet appear what we shall be: but we know that, when he shall appear, we shall be like him; for we shall see Him as He is" (I John 3:2).*

Think of it this way: We are seeds, and it is hard to tell what we will look like when we bloom. Unless you are an expert in horticulture, when you look at a seed, you do not know what the tree or plant will look like.

But without being a farmer, you do know that a seed will reproduce after its kind. So all we have to do is plant the seed and wait until God gets through with it. Then we will see exactly what it is. Otherwise, you will not know the difference between a turnip seed and a collard seed. You cannot discern the difference between a red pepper seed and a green pepper seed. But when God gets through with it, you can see the difference.

Jesus presented a parable stating, *"The kingdom of heaven is like a mustard seed, which a man took and sowed in his field; and this is smaller than all other seeds; but when it is full grown, it is larger than the garden plants, and becomes a tree, so that the birds of the air come and nest in its branches"* (Matt. 13:31-32 NAS). You may start off like that tiny mustard seed. But before God is through with you, He builds a mighty tree in you as a refuge to others. So learn not to measure yourself by where you have been or where you are. Instead, measure yourself by where you are going, because God is not through with you yet!

After Job lost everything he had, he could have easily come to the conclusion that God was finished in his life. But when you think of Job, you think of a man who is known for patience and endurance. In the midst of Job's trials and frustrations, he said, *"But he knoweth the way that I take: when He hath tried me, I SHALL COME FORTH AS GOLD"* (Job 23:10). Even when Job was down in his circumstances, he was not down in his outlook! Job was not looking where he was. He was looking where he was going! He did not see his life as black and dismal; he saw gold! That ought to teach us something! **When you see black, look for the gold!** The gold will not just jump in your hands. You have to get up and dig for it!

Down in his spirit, Job knew God would work everything for good in his life. Job knew that God was not through with him. How did he know this? Because he was not through with God! In his trial, Job remained faithful to God. Job knew God had something more for him. This is why he could remain faithful! He knew that his course was not finished. You see, immediately after Job said, "I shall come forth as gold," he said, *"My foot hath held His steps, His way have I kept, and not declined. Neither have I gone back from the commandment of His lips; I have esteemed the words of His mouth more than my necessary food" (Job 23:11-12).* Because Job refused to release God, **God could not leave him. God had to bless Job because it is His nature to reward faithfulness!**

If you have fallen or failed in any area of your life, do not despair. You were not the first to fall, and you will not be the last. If you have fallen, all you need is a fresh start. That is what repentance does for us. It gives us a fresh start with God. I liken it to the fact that the sun goes down every day. All the failures and bad experiences can be left in that day. Then in the morning, we have a fresh start! It is a new day, a day to be better and to do better.

No matter how hard or how low you have fallen, you can get up and move on! Moses fell when he killed an Egyptian, but that marked the beginning of God's using him. Abraham fell when he laid with Hagar who bore

Ishmael, a wild man. Yet, God was just beginning to bring about the promised child, Isaac. Think about Samson. He fell by telling a woman his secret and breaking his covenant with God. As a result, his hair was shaved and his eyes were gouged out. Still, the Lord accomplished a greater judgment through Samson's death than he did in his life.

After King David sinned with Bathsheba, he thought it was over for him. But God brought correction to him and restored his life. And the list goes on. So when you have fallen and you cannot get up, look up and call on the Lord. He will hear your cry and restore you. Remember, *"For the Son of man is come to seek and to save that which was lost" (Luke 19:10)*. If you have fallen or strayed from the Lord, someone very special is looking for you! He wants you to get up and move on!

CHAPTER 11
Free At Last

"If you are bound by certain disconcerting habits, you need to know truth to help you break that habit. Jesus very aptly said, "And ye shall know the truth, and the truth shall make you free." (John 8:32)

To hear a life-changing message does not change your life. To read a life-changing story does not change your life. To witness life-changing experiences does not change your life. What changes your life is **truth!**

Truth, when applied to your life, can change you for the better and forever. If you are bound by certain disconcerting habits, you need to know the truth to help you break that habit. Jesus very aptly said, *"And ye shall know the truth, and the truth shall make you free" (John 8:32).* You see, the dope addict suffers with compulsive behavior. But the truth is that within that dope addict is a person of worth. The truth is that within every alcoholic, there is a person of sobriety. Within every overeater, there is a person of moderation. Within every perverted person, there is someone of sound moral values. However, if we do not know the truth of what truly lies within, we cannot change the exterior.

Hidden truth, just like hidden treasure, is of no value. If you do not know a truth, you cannot act on it. Then, if you do not act on a truth, it has no power to bring change in your life. Truth is not generally on the surface. You must dig for it. Truth, you see, is discovered or uncovered — not stumbled upon.

Everything is minuscule compared to truth that is realized in your life. For every area of bondage in life, there is a corresponding truth that delivers freedom from that bondage. Despite the negative experiences of your past, present truth can make you free! In spite of the fears of your future, present truth can make you free! What lies in you is far more efficacious than what lies behind you or before you! When you realize that truth, you will be set free.

A few years ago, a middle-aged woman came to me and said, "I'm scared to go in certain parts of my house. I live alone." I asked, "How long have you been living alone?" She replied, "Ever since my husband died, four years ago." Then I asked, "Did you ever have this fear while your husband was living?" "Of course not," she responded "because I knew my husband wouldn't let anything bad happen to me!" I began to explain, "Now the Lord is your husband. He is your protector and provider. He will not let anything bad happen to you!" With a pensive expression, she raised her eyebrows as if to say, "I never thought of it like that before." I corroborated with Scripture what I told her. Then I asked her, "Do you know what the Bible says to you in the 13th chapter of Hebrews?" She looked puzzled. "It says," I continued,

"... I will never leave thee, nor forsake thee. So that we may boldly say, The Lord is my helper, and I will not fear what man shall do unto me."

Hebrews 13:5b-6

Before I could finish quoting the verse, this middle-aged woman had both arms in the air. Tears began to roll down her cheeks. With a trembling voice she cried, "Lord, I know you are with me! You've brought me this far, and I know you will take care of me!"

She already knew the truth of what I shared with her. She just was not walking in that truth. So, you see, **practicing the truth** is a part of knowing the truth. We cannot neglect that part of knowing truth. To know truth, without doing that truth, is ignorance!

Ignorance is simply disregarding or ignoring what you know to be truth.

After a month passed, I ran into this woman again. The first thing she said to me was, "I used to think it was better to be scared than dead. But now I know it is better to live free and have glee." She was beaming from ear to ear. She told me, "Ever since you shared that Scripture with me, I have not been afraid to go in my basement nor my attic." "In fact," she continued, "I cleaned my entire basement last Friday **night!**" Now what happened to this woman? Did all the threat of fear just leave her life? No. **The truth that God was with her superseded her fear.** I rejoiced with this woman because I could see the truth had made her free!

About a year and a half later, I saw this same lady again. I went over to her in the grocery store and asked, "How are you doing?" She said, "I've been doing fine, except for one thing — that fear of going in certain parts of my house has come back on me." She recalled, "I was doing fine until about three months ago. I looked at a scary movie, about a haunted house one night, and I have been scared ever since." She went on, "At night, my house gets real spooky. My imagination runs away with me..." I interrupted to ask, "Do you remember the Scripture I gave you that set you free the first time?" She said, "I believe it was something about the Lord being with me and never leaving me." I said, "That's the one!" Then I challenged her saying, "Start reciting that Scripture everyday and the fear will abate as confidence will abound!" She took the challenge and started practicing what I told her. After four years, she told me, "I'm still free because of that truth you taught me to confess in my life everyday!" As long as she walks in that truth, she will remain free.

You see, **the key is not in knowing the truth; it is in practicing the truth.** Yes, Jesus indubitably stated, "Ye shall know the truth, and the truth shall make you free." But there is a prerequisite to that statement. In the verse before that Jesus clarified, *"If ye continue in my word, then are ye my disciples indeed" (John 8:31b).* So, you see, the key to knowing the truth is **continuing in the Word!** When you hear truth, do not just get excited and shout all over the place. Listen to that truth. Write it down. Get it down in your spirit. Memorize it. Confess it. Determine ways you can put that truth into practice in your life. Too many times, we get so excited when we hear good truth that we just go into a frenzy and drop the truth on the floor. Then the words of Isaiah come to life:

Therefore is judgment far from us, neither doth justice overtake us: we wait for light, but behold obscurity; for brightness, but we walk in darkness ... For our transgressions are multiplied before thee, and our sins testify against us: for our transgressions are with us; and as for our iniquities, we know them ... And judgment is turned away backward, and justice standeth afar off: for truth is fallen in the street, and equity cannot enter.
          Isaiah 59:9,12,14

If you do not take the truth that you hear and run, it will fall dormantly to the streets. Truth is given to be practiced! It is only when we practice truth that true freedom is experienced.

You may have been miraculously healed, delivered or set free, but it takes truth to keep you free! Miracles, signs and wonders can get you free, but there is no guarantee you will remain free! If you are set free through a gift of the Holy Spirit or by the sovereignty of God, you still need the Word of God in your life to keep you free! Sometimes only God can set you free, but only you can keep yourself free by continuing in the truth of the Word of God.

I have seen innumerable cases of individuals that experienced a genuine deliverance and were set free. Yet a large percentage of them had relapses. Those who have relapses often feel the system failed. They think, "That drug rehabilitation program just wasn't for me." They say or feel, "I obviously didn't get enough in my counseling session." Others who were delivered by supernatural means feel, "I guess I wasn't delivered after all." But the truth is that there was nothing wrong with the system or the counseling or the miracle. The problem is that the individual did not **continue** in the discipline of the system. The person did not follow the guidance of the counselor. He did not **continue** in the Word of the Lord.

You see, we love any kind of panacea that can fix us once and for all. We do not want the responsibility of **"continuing"** on our shoulders. When the doctor gives you a prescription, there are certain instructions that come with it. If you intend to ameliorate your health, you will follow the instructions for your medication. But you must continue with it, if you want the result of better health. "Continuing" is a process that keeps our life in good shape.

Paul, writing to the Church at Ephesus, mentioned that Christ loved the Church and gave himself for it *"that he might sanctify and cleanse it with the washing of water by the word" (Ephesians 5:26).* Well, you see, continuing in the Word is like taking a bath. If you do not regularly wash yourself, you will begin to stink. If you do not wash yourself, rancid odors will defile your being. No matter how good your soap is, I guarantee that it will not last a lifetime. No matter how long you stay in the shower or tub, there will come a time real soon when you will need another washing.

As you continue in the Word of the Lord, your life is washed and the putrid scent leaves. **Coming to God's Word brings information, reformation and transformation. But departing from His Word causes deformation, demoralization and degeneration.** So if you want to keep your life fresh and clean, you must stay in the Word. When you leave the church service, continue in the Word! While you are on the job, continue in the Word! While in your home, continue in the Word! When you go on vacation, continue in the Word! **Wherever you are, continue in the Word!** By continuing in the Word, you will know the truth, and **the truth will make you free!** Then, AND when the truth makes you free, you are free at last!

A young man, with whom I am acquainted, grew up without a father. He often wondered who his father was. He wanted to know what he looked like. There were many unanswered questions. When he was about

23 years old, his mother finally told him who his real father was. She told him exactly where he lived. So the young man, whom I will call Billy, drove to his father's house. He was afraid to just go up to the door and say, "Hi, dad." So he inconspicuously sat in his car across the street from his father's house. With his heart beating fiercely with anticipation, he noticed every car that came up the street. With every male driver, he wondered, "Is that my dad?" Finally, one turned into the driveway of his father's address. Unobtrusively looking at this stately man, Billy knew this was his father. He knew his father worked for the government and wore a uniform. Just to see his father in the flesh answered a myriad of questions that had plagued his mind for years. Feeling too awkward to approach his father, he sped off without saying anything.

Weeks later Billy built up enough courage to introduce himself to his father. Because of pictures that the mother had sent, the father knew exactly who Billy was. Although Billy's father had a wife and children, the two of them endeavored to build a relationship. It was a success. The truth made the young man free, and accepting that truth will keep him free forever. Now, Billy knows that his father loves him and approves of him. Now he is free to be a man! The truth made the young man free, and accepting that truth will keep him free forever.

You see, truth will make you free to be who you are and what God has called you to be! Continue in the Word, and it will bring light and understanding to you. You will soon know truth, and those truths you learn and practice will make and keep you free! Then you will be **free at last!**

O R D E R   F O R M

Bronner Books are available from Century Systems at quantity discount for ministries, institutions, schools, businesses, and other organizations. For more information, call or write to: Century Systems Inc., Box 43725, Atlanta, GA 30336 1-800-843-9662.

You may send letters to the author at the above address, your letters will be forwarded.

Fax orders (404) 696-2480
Visa/MC orders (24hrs/day) call 1-800-843-9662
internet e-mail sales@thewoman.com
full text of books are online at www.thewoman.com
Check or Money Order orders mail to:
Century Systems, Box 43725, Atlanta, GA 30336

Please send me the following number of copies of Bronner books at 9.95 ea. plus 2.00 ea p&h:

Qty	Title	ISBN#
_____	**Get A Grip**	**0-9631075-2-6**
_____	**Just For The Asking**	**0-9631075-3-4**
_____	**Quick Fasting**	**0-9631075-1-8**
_____	**How To Find God**	**0-9631075-5-0**

Total Number of books _____   x9.95 ea. = _____

Total Number of books _____   x 2.00 p&h= _____

☐**Ck/MO enclosed**   ☐ **Visa/MC**   **Total** _____

(Georgia residents add tax)

Please RUSH my books to: (Please Print)

Name _____

Address _____

City_____ **State**_____ **Zip**_____

Visa/MC#_____ **Exp** _____

Signature_____

VISA/MC ORDERS CALL TOLL FREE 24 HOURS A DAY
1-800-THE-WOMAN   1-800-843-9662